A MAP OF MENTAL STATES

John H. Clark
MA, MB (Cantab.), DPM

A MAP OF
MENTAL
STATES

Foreword by
Gordon Pask

Routledge & Kegan Paul
London, Boston, Melbourne and Henley

First published in 1983
by Routledge & Kegan Paul plc
39 Store Street, London WC1E 7DD,
9 Park Street, Boston, Mass. 02108, USA,
296 Beaconsfield Parade, Middle Park,
Melbourne, 3206, Australia, and
Broadway House, Newtown Road,
Henley-on-Thames, Oxon RG9 1EN
Set in Sabon by
Rowland Phototypesetting Ltd, Bury St Edmunds, Suffolk
and printed in Great Britain by
St Edmundsbury Press, Bury St Edmunds, Suffolk
© John H. Clark 1983

Library of Congress Cataloging in Publication Data

Clark, John H., 1929–
A map of mental states.
Bibliography: p.
Includes index.
1. Consciousness. I. Title. [DNLM: 1. Mysticism.
2.   Psychology.   BF 38 C593m]
BF311.C542   1983   150   82–20467

ISBN 0-7100-9235-0

Man has his country, the geography of his personal self.
Rabindranath Tagore

Contents

Figures

Tables

Tables

Foreword

John Clark is a very old friend and colleague. We have but one bone of contention, and that is his delay in bringing the ideas, described in this book, to press and general availability. A perfectionist, Clark has maintained a need to polish, furbish and further scrutinize his conception of a map representing a space of mental states before setting it down, except in personal memoranda and a few hard-to-obtain papers and conference proceedings.

Upon reading the manuscript, I feel Clark was right to be tardy. The exposition is altogether more lucid than the-already-valuable, earlier essays. Also, it was probably necessary for him to return to Cambridge for a year, on study leave, in order to crystallize notions which originated, albeit in an embryonic form, whilst he was in residence at the university some 30 years ago. For it is the elegance of the whole thing that renders the parts cohesive and, in fact, gives significance to the odd interstices between domains of mental activity.

Any psychiatrist, practitioner or teacher, must have a means of navigation and some way of charting position upon the territory of the mind. Some use words connected in a graph-like structure; others use pictures of interlocking control systems, often relating mood and awareness to physiological conditions or patterns of overt behaviour.

Clark has a very complicated model for state of mind; it could be a theory. At least it is a model, tried and supported by reference to literature, as well as by individual studies. It is of wider-than-usual span and includes meditational, religious, depressive and euphoric conditions. However, this (model, nearly-a-theory, of a space of mental states) was far too complicated, as it stood, to be of much practical value.

Therefore, by way of ingenious compromise, Clark has projected his underlying framework upon a geometrical three-dimensional space (in much the same way that visual perception involves a projection of a three, or more, dimensional space onto the two-dimensional retinae, from which apparition the brain constructs an always ambiguous, but everyday usable, image of objects in what we call three-dimensional space). Clark's choice of bi-conical space turns out to be extraordinarily fruitful and to have, in terms of the trajectories traversing it, explanatory power.

There is one major singularity (Thom or Zeeman would call it a 'catastrophe set', in the language of 'Catastrophe Theory'), and there are various conditional singularities. Hence, it is propitious to ordain a plane surface, with the major singularity at its centre, cutting the conical projections in half; moreover, to project trajectories (series of states of mind) onto the even more readily usable two-dimensional plane.

Apart from the scholarship of the book and the careful clinical-type research, Clark's innovation is twofold. First, the choice of a manageable and, incidentally, beautiful, geometrical representation; next the ability to retrieve (obviously, with ambiguity, but with apparent success) the information necessarily lost by any projection, and thereby explore trajectories of mood, awareness and apprehension which characterize the flux of mental events.

To me, the book is illuminating, and I believe that other readers will find it so. It is to be hoped that this book is one of a series expressing the ideas, as well as the acumen, of an original, cautious and insightful thinker.

Gordon Pask
Richmond upon Thames

Preface

This book first arose out of an attempt to explain the mystical literature to myself. I felt that mystical language was a code and I wanted to 'crack' it. Gradually, I found myself drawing a map of the mystical path.

However, as I worked, I found that I was really working on a larger map, a map of the mind, a *map* of mental states. What is more, as the work continued, I seemed to be gaining more insight into other topics, such as mental illness, mythology and religion.

A dialogue had been set up between the *map* and myself, and my efforts to record it have produced this book.

J.H.C.

Acknowledgments

The present book is a much-expanded version of my chapter in *Six Approaches to the Person*, published by Routledge & Kegan Paul in 1972 and edited by my colleague Ralph Ruddock.

I owe a great many thanks to Mr Ruddock. He encouraged my early efforts to draw my *map*, prompted me to give extra-mural lectures on it and has since given me unfailing encouragement.

Work-in-progress on the *map* was published in the medical newspaper *Pulse* and I am grateful to its medical editor, Dr Hertzel Creditor.

The following have kindly supplied me with information about films and television programmes: The British Film Institute, Mr David Quinland of the *TV Times*, and Mr Eric Rhodes.

Work began on the *map* in about 1964 when I was an MRC Clinical Research Fellow in the Department of Psychology at the University of Bristol. It continued when I was at the former MRC Psycholinguistics Research Unit at the University of Oxford in 1966. Since 1967 I have been in the Department of Psychology at the University of Manchester under Professor Emeritus John Cohen, Professor James Reason and Professor M. Sebastian Halliday. The academic year 1980–1 was spent on study leave at the University of Cambridge, with Dr Martin Richards at the Child Care and Development Group (formerly the Medical Psychology Unit), where I completed the present book.

The *map* has gradually emerged from a continuous process of reading and thinking. This has been interspersed with discussions with many colleagues at Manchester and else-where, and with innumerable undergraduate, postgraduate and extra-mural students. In particular, my former colleague Dr Alan N. Fish has given me a great deal of help and constructive criticism. Among other things, he suggested the use of a second cone, so as to make one on-line and the other off-line; and the way of classifying ineffability in terms of a communication channel. He also wrote the computer graphics program which forms Appendix I.

I am very grateful to my old friend and scientific mentor, Professor Gordon Pask, who has kindly written the Foreword.

Section 12.3 owes much to my conversations with the Rev. Dr David Doel when he was writing his thesis (Doel, 1973).

Section 5.3 is based on discussions with my colleague Mr Lance Cousins, with whom I also had many discussions about Patanjali.

I also wish to thank the following for giving me their critical comments on various chapters: my former senior colleague Dr Peter Brook, my colleague Dr J. P. Kane and my colleague Dr J. M. H. Rees. The entire book was scrutinized meticulously by Miss Christine Hubbert and Dr Alan N. Fish.

I hope I may be forgiven for any omissions in the following list, which is of the many other people to whom I also owe thanks: Dr Philip S. Alexander, Dr Michael Apter, Dr Paul Arnold, Professor Stafford Beer, Dr Clifford Bell, Mr G. Spencer Brown, Mr Michael D. M. Butterworth, Mr Eric Chesnick, Dr Ian P. Christensen, Mr Oliver J. Clark, Mr W. Glyn Davies, Professor John A. Davis, Mr Nicholas Doran, Mr Upali Ekanayaka, Mr Christopher Ellison, Dr C. M. Elstob, Mr Peter Eserin, Mr Malcolm Evison, Mr Adrian Gaggs, Mr Alan Gardner, Mr Alan Garman, Professor Frank H. George, Mr Vernon A. J. Gifford, Mr Kevin Gillespie, Mrs Margaret Gissop, Dr Per Hage, Mr Sam Hart, Mr George Hay, Mr Glen Heller, Dr Nils Holm, Dr John Howarth, Mr Oliver Hunt, Mr Galen Ives, Dr A. R. W. James, Professor F. A. Jenner, Miss Judy Lawrence, Mr Harry Lesser, Mr Grevel Lindop, Dr Malcolm McCausland, Mr Ian MacNab, Mr G. S. Mani, Dr Andrew Mayes, Mr David Melling, Mr Martin Miles, the Rev. Roy Moore, Professor John F. Morris, Mr Richard Nash, Miss Deborah Noah, Professor Akio Ono, Mr Francis

Parkinson, Dr Kenneth Pease, Mr D. T. J. Pedley, Dr Ivor Pleydell-Pearce, Dr Harry Rothman, Dr Eric Rutter, Mr Timothy St Ather, Mr John W. Shaw, Dr Paul H. Spriggs, Dr David J. Stewart, Dr Paul Stewart, Mr Andrew Swales, Dr Tom Whiston, Dr John Wilson, Professor Arthur Wingfield, the Rev. Canon Frank S. Wright and Dr Vladimir Zakian.

I should also like to thank the following for permission to quote copyright material:
Oxford University Press, Oxford, for an excerpt from 'Centuries of Meditation' by Thomas Traherne. Quoted by F. C. Happold, 1963; Penguin Books Ltd for an excerpt from al-Ghazali, 'Mishkat al-Anwar', reprinted from F. C. Happold, *Mysticism* (Penguin Books, Revised edition, 1970), p. 99. Copyright © F. C. Happold, 1963, 1964, 1970; Arthur Koestler and The Macmillan Co., New York, for three short extracts from *The Invisible Writing*, 1954. Copyright © Arthur Koestler, 1954 (A. D. Peters & Co. Ltd, Writers' Agents). Quoted in Stace, 1960; John Blofeld, George Allen & Unwin, Ltd., London, and E. P. Dutton, Inc., New York, for Diagram 4 from *The Way of Power*, p. 120. Copyright © George Allen & Unwin Ltd, 1970; Curtis Brown Ltd, Macmillan, London and Basingstoke, and Charles Scribner's Sons, New York, for an extract from *Corridors of Power*, by C. P. Snow (Penguin, Harmondsworth, 1966). Copyright © Philip A. Snow and Edmund A. Williams-Ashman, 1964; Frederick Ungar Publishing Co., New York for an extract from *The Dark Night of the Soul*, by St John of the Cross, 1957 edn. Quoted by W. T. Stace, 1960; Little, Brown & Co., Boston, Mass., for an extract from *The Journal* of Charles Marshall, 1844, quoted by Anne Fremantle in *The Protestant Mystics*, Mentor, New York, 1964; Thames & Hudson Ltd and Pantheon Books, a Division of Random House, Inc. for an extract from Chuang Tzu, quoted by Alan Watts, in *The Way of Zen*, Penguin, 1957; Editions Gallimard for excerpts from *Nausea* by Jean-Paul Sartre, © Editions Gallimard, 1938 (trans., Penguin, 1970); Roland Fischer and John Wiley & Sons, Inc., New York, for Figure 3 from Chapter 6 in Siegel, R. K. and West, L. J., *Hallucinations: Behaviour, Experience, and Theory*, John Wiley, 1975.

Introduction

Maps of the mind

This book describes a *map* of mental states, a *map* of the mind. Various maps of the mind have been drawn by previous authors, but the present map tries to be more systematic and more comprehensive. I hope that it will be interesting to psychologists and physicians, and stimulating to reflective people in general.

An ordinary map, such as the familiar 'one inch to the mile' Ordnance Survey map, or its metric equivalent, is basically a picture of part of the world; but a very small picture, because it uses only one inch on the map to portray a mile on the ground. Nevertheless one can 'read' such a map and recreate quite a good picture, in one's head, of the terrain that it represents. Similarly, my own *map* of the mind represents a large amount of information crowded into a very small space. Also, like other maps, it uses a number of symbols or 'conventional signs'.

The advantage of maps is that they sum up a lot of information in a greatly reduced form which can then be assimilated quickly. By contrast, their disadvantage is that many things in the region being mapped cannot be included on the particular map. Such things must be omitted altogether or greatly simplified. Thus, for example, the 'one inch' Ordnance Survey map sometimes shows individual houses, but when it does so it omits all their details such as their windows, doors and roofs. It only shows black spots, to indicate their position. Again, a wood around a group of such houses is reduced to a few simplified tree-symbols.

The same factors apply to my *map* of mental states. It has to omit or simplify most of the enormous complexity of the mind, and yet this disadvantage is accompanied by the corresponding advantage that it enables one to 'take in' a mental state, or a series of mental states, 'at a glance'.

Definitions

I mean by 'mind' the whole range of mental states, i.e. of conscious states, sleeping and waking, which a person can experience. My *map* tries to display them on the surface of a cone. There are also various paths on the cone which show some of the routes that can be taken by people, from one mental state to another, 'through' their own minds.

By 'mental state' I mean the values taken by a person's set of 'main' mental variables at any particular time. Such main variables include excitement, general mood (pleasant or unpleasant), intensity of general mood, concentration, and so on.

In mental illnesses particularly, various other, 'extra', mental variables, including various symptoms, show themselves, such as false or distorted perceptions (hallucinations and illusions), delusions, phobias, obsessions and compulsions, and so on. The hallucinogenic drugs such as mescaline and LSD, and other kinds of drug, also cause characteristic symptoms.

However, even in 'ordinary life' a person can experience a very wide range of values of the main mental variables and a wide selection of extra variables. For example, ordinary life contains all the 'ups and downs' of our daily work and leisure. It also contains orgasms and toothaches, daydreams and nightmares, anger and laughter.

My aim, therefore, in this book, is to draw a *map* on which enough variables can be displayed to indicate some of the range of the mind in both health and sickness, i.e. I want to cover not only ordinary life but also the unusual life of the mystics, the abnormal life of the mentally ill and the 'artificial life' of the takers of some drugs, especially the hallucinogens.

The mental variables on the *map* are subjective, and also either ordinal or binary. We infer the value of those of others from their behaviour, which includes what they say.

Philosophical assumptions

In order to write this book I have had to assume that, in general, other people's minds at least resemble my own. I also assume that the descriptions of their minds that people give us, verbally or in writing, are true. However, there are drawbacks to this latter assumption, in that some people probably tell lies about their minds. I expect, therefore, that I am taken in occasionally.

On the other hand, only I myself know if my own description of my own mind is true or not, or indeed if I even have a mind at all. Similarly, I do not know for sure if other people have minds. In everyday life I act on the assumption that they do, and that is what I do in this book.

The mystics as psychologists

In Chapter 1 I talk about mental states in ordinary life. Then in Chapter 2 I discuss the mental territory described by the mystics. This is an unusual region, but one of my positive reasons for studying the mystics is that I see them as an informal but determined group of applied psychologists. They repeatedly experiment upon themselves and observe the changes in their mental states which result; that is to say, they perform mystical procedures, notably meditation, which take them into unusual regions of their minds. What is more, provided they stick fairly closely to the methods laid down by their various traditions, then the mystics need not get too confused as to where they are. True, they may get slightly lost from time to time, but their traditions guide them back again onto the 'mystical path'. The descriptions they have given us and continue to give us – for there are mystics in every age and every culture – show some noticeable common features and it is these that led me to draw my first tentative maps.

Another reason for studying the mystics is that the mystical path has several points which are useful as landmarks, where the mental state changes dramatically. Some of these may also be encountered in mental illnesses and after taking the hallucinogenic drugs, but the descriptions, then, are not so clear as those of the mystics.

Lastly, the mystical path contains several stages which pass through ordinary life itself; put another way, ordinary life is itself on the mystical path. Mental illnesses and drug states, on the other hand, are slightly off the mystical path, although connected to it by byways.

The plan of the book

Having drawn a chart of the mystical path in Chapter 2, I describe the *map* as a whole in Chapter 3. Then, in the remainder of the book, I use the *map* to plot some of the journeys through ordinary life, mystical states, mental illnesses and various drug states. I also discuss mythology and the arts. I then trace the evolution of the *map*.

Underlying all these explorations is the simple geometrical shape of the *map*, i.e. a cone with various lines drawn upon its curved surface or projected down onto its base.

Summary of this Introduction

Maps are useful because they present a lot of information at a glance. It should, therefore, be useful to present a description of a person's mental state in the form of a map. However, maps in general have to omit some details and simplify others, using 'conventional signs'. The *map* in this book does both. It aims to be comprehensive, in its coverage of a wide variety of mental states. Like a geographical map, it has co-ordinates or dimensions. These are rather similar to the lines of latitude and longitude on a terrestrial globe.

PART ONE

Main sources
of the *map*

In this part of the book I present the two sources from which I obtained the main features of the *map*. In Chapter 1 I consider the mental states that occur in such variety in ordinary life. Then in Chapter 2 I discuss mysticism, analysing mystical states, mystical 'procedures' and what I call the 'problem of mysticism'.

There are, of course, other sources on which I have drawn when devising the *map*. In particular, the striking polarities between pleasant and unpleasant states in both mental illnesses and hallucinogenic drug states. Nevertheless, the main sources are the two discussed in this part of the book.

Chapter 1

Mental states in ordinary life

The term 'ordinary life' covers an extraordinary range of different mental states and it is only our familiarity with them which conceals this fact from us.

Some of the ideas contained in this chapter may be rather obvious to the reader, but I have to set them out carefully in order to lay a firm foundation for what follows.

1.1 Main variables of the *map*

I am now going to introduce all the main variables of the *map*. I shall do so informally, presenting them in the way that we experience them in ordinary life.

They will be discussed again in Chapter 2 and then they will be used, in Chapter 3, to help construct the *map*.

Mind work

We notice, during both waking and sleeping, that there are fluctuations in our level of mental alertness, or 'mental energy'. I call this variable mind work. I think that when it is at an ordinary, 'average' level we do not notice it. However, we do notice it when it falls to a low level of lethargy or drowsiness, or when it rises to a high level of unusual alertness or excitement. The equivalent of mind work, in terms of brain physiology, is what is called 'general arousal' (Berlyne, 1969). This can be envisaged as a general mobilization of the brain, so that it is ready to do whatever is required of it. 'When arousal is high, our senses are alerted and our reactions, both mental and physical, are at their height' (Wingfield and Byrnes, 1981).

General mood and intensity of general mood

We can usually say that our general mood is either pleasant or unpleasant. It also varies in intensity. However, at ordinary, 'average' levels of intensity, unless we are in an unpleasant general mood, I do not think we notice our mood very much, and so, if asked, find it hard to say whether it is pleasant or not.

Nevertheless, I assume that such unselfconscious, average states of ordinary life are in fact on the 'pleasant' side. My reasons for doing so will gradually emerge as I put the *map* together.

It follows, however, from the above assumption that an average state of intensity of an unpleasant general mood is, by contrast, definitely noticeable. My overall idea is that such states are fairly rare but do occur; for example, in 'hangovers' after alcoholic excess, or in the unpleasant recovery phase from virus illnesses such as influenza. People then say that they do not feel well, that they feel 'heavy' or 'out of sorts', that they are suffering from 'malaise'.

Aspects of mind

An important idea, which I will build into the *map* itself, is that as one's general mood changes from pleasant to unpleasant, or vice versa, and also as it changes in intensity from average levels to low or high ones, a whole set of other mental functions or 'aspects of mind' change with it. They all become affected at the same time and to the same degree. This is a large assumption but I find it very useful when drawing the *map*.

The above-mentioned set of aspects of mind are expressed by the mystics in terms of: Knowledge, Unity and Eternity; Light and Body sense; Joy; and Freedom. They involve cognition, perception, emotion and volition. They will be discussed further in Chapter 2. They are brought into prominence by the high intensity states of the mystics. The aspects of mind are not so obvious when intensity is at average levels, especially when the general mood is pleasant, but if our intensity changes to high or low or our general mood changes to unpleasant, or both, then we become more aware of the details of our mental state and can distinguish our different aspects more clearly.

On-line and off-line functions

Sometimes we interact with our environment: seeing, hearing, smelling and feeling it; or doing things in or to it, such as talking to people, or walking about and lifting things. To use an engineering term, we are then 'on-line', in the sense that we are exchanging information or energy, or both, with our environment. That is to say, we are connected with it in two directions, sending and receiving messages or physical objects both to and from it.

At other times we seem to be mainly, if not entirely, 'off-line', having retreated within ourselves to think about a problem or to remember something or just to daydream.

In practice, I think that we are nearly always, to some extent, both on-line and off-line, and I envisage both functions as being dealt with by separate parts of the mind, but at the same time. When we daydream, and even when we dream at night, we continue to monitor our environment with our on-line function, so that we can respond to it if some important message reaches us.

'Daydreaming' is an ambiguous term because we can, when mainly off-line, be concentrating very hard indeed on some problem, or mental image, or fantasy. On the other hand we can be in a vague (and 'dream-like') state which we find hard to recall if, for example, offered 'a penny for our thoughts'. I am using 'dream-like' here to describe the quality possessed by most, but not all, night dreams. It is a vague, elusive quality.

It is possible to be in a vague daydream when one is also interacting, if only slightly, with the environment, on-line. In this case the daydream itself is mainly off-line but may be given little prods now and then from the outside world. An example of this occurs at the end of the first chapter of C. P. Snow's novel, *Corridors of Power* (1964):

(The narrator and his wife are dropping off a friend, David, after a dinner party.)
   The taxi throbbed along the Embankment towards Chelsea . . .
   . . . as I gazed out of the window I did not join in much. I let myself drift into a kind of daydream.

When we had said good night to David, Margaret took my hand.

'What are you thinking about?' she said.
I couldn't tell her. I was just staring out at the comfortable familiar town. The Chelsea back-streets, which I used to know, the lights of Fulham Road; Kensington squares; the stretch of Queen's Gate up towards the Park. All higgledy-piggledy, leafy, not pretty, nearer the ground than the other capital cities. I was not exactly remembering, although much had happened to me there; but I had a sense, not sharp, of joys hidden about the place, of love, of marriage, of miseries and elations, of coming out into the night air. The talk after dinner had not come back to my mind; it was one of many; we were used to them. And yet, I felt vulnerable, as if soft with tenderness towards the town itself, although in cold blood I should not have said that I liked it overmuch.

The idea of the storage of a skill in the memory can be introduced briefly here. For example, motorists are familiar with the experience of driving long distances and being efficiently on-line all the way, alert to their own behaviour and to that of other drivers and pedestrians. However, they are also familiar with their own surprised realization that sometimes, at the end of the journey, especially if it is a well-known route, they cannot recall much of it other than starting out and arriving at their destination. They have been on-line and were using adequate mind work, but the whole exercise was already such a skilled one, and stored ready for use, that this latest performance of it was not retained as a separate memory and cannot therefore be recalled.

However, should some event have occurred during the journey that required extra mind work or extra concentration, then the driver can probably recall it at the end of the journey. Such an event might have been an unexpected diversion due to a bridge being widened.

Sleeping or waking

We all know that our mental states when asleep, i.e. our dreams, are in some way different from our mental states when we are awake, although there are also similarities. It is, however, very difficult to say just what this difference is. One reason for this is that we usually forget our dreams and therefore cannot study them. Indeed, unless a person gets into the habit of recording his dreams as soon as he wakes up he may firmly believe that he doesn't dream at all.

Throughout sleep there are periods of rapid eye movements (REM) during which we have vivid dreams, but at other times during sleep no dreams occur at all, or only ones that resemble, ordinary, waking thinking (see Oswald, 1970; Hartman, 1973).

The general mood of a dream can be pleasant or unpleasant and its intensity can vary widely. Dreams can also be excited or lethargic, that is to say, they can vary in mind work.

The content of dreams, the actual things that we dream, is usually related to the events of the day or two preceding the period of sleep in question.

A dreamer can know that he is dreaming, and such dreams have been called lucid dreams (Green, 1968). Some dreams are recurrent and are recognized as such by the dreamer, although I am not sure whether this recognition occurs on waking or during the dream, or both.

The logic of events during a dream may not be very different from that of every day, or it may be quite different. This latter quality has always appealed to some creative people. Indeed the Surrealists, such as Max Ernst, Marcel Duchamp, Salvador Dali and René Magritte, borrow its strange magic for their paintings and sculpture.

From a state of sleep we can be awakened with varying degrees of difficulty. Part of our mind can therefore be envisaged as monitoring the external world for messages important enough to rouse us from sleep. This part of the mind remains on-line to the world, just active enough to detect these messages. The rest of our mind performs different functions. It is off-line and is engaged, for some of the time at least during sleep, in dreaming.

Concentration of attention
We are aware, sometimes, that we are both concentrating
our attention upon things and that we are doing more mind
work. Alternatively, if we are concentrating without doing
more mind work, we may be doing so by focusing our attention on fewer things.

We pay more attention to something when we want to
observe it more carefully, as when we look at or feel the shape
of a coin to make sure that it is, say, a fifty-pence piece and not
a ten-pence piece. Or we may pay more attention when we
come across something we enjoy, such as a particular work of
art or a real landscape.

Attention and things
Attention itself is a sort of mental currency. We 'pay' attention
to things. Sometimes we are asked to pay more attention to one
thing and less to another. When we pay a lot of attention to a
few things we are conscious of concentrating our attention on
them.

Sometimes we are overwhelmed by things and become
muddled. This happens when we cannot grasp the things
sufficiently to sort them out, so as to deal with them properly
and thus to cope with them. If this happens we are aware that
we must exert more mind work or concentrate our attention
more, or both, in order to 'get a grip' on things again, to get
things under control.

We find it harder to concentrate our attention when we are
tired, bored or anxious.

Diffusion of attention
When our attention is low in comparison with the number of
things to which it is being paid, I call it 'diffuse' as opposed to
concentrated. Our attention is then being diffused over many
things rather than concentrated on a few.

1.2 Main variables and extra variables
In the last section the main variables were described briefly in
their relation to ordinary life. They are shown in Table 1.1.

Table 1.1 The main variables

Mind work
General mood: pleasant or unpleasant
Intensity of general mood and aspects of mind
On-line and off-line functions
Sleeping or waking
Concentration and diffusion of attention
Attention and things

These are the variables which will be built, step by step, into the structure of the *map* as it is assembled in Chapter 3. They will be described in greater detail later. Some are binary (i.e. two-valued) variables, others are continuous. There is some overlap between them because attention and things, together, are related to mind work and concentration (or diffusion) of attention, as discussed in Chapter 3.

However, the variety and subtlety of mental life cannot be encompassed on a map formed from the above variables alone. I am obliged to add extra variables as they are required in the captions to the figures. This is the same policy as that adopted by terrestrial map-makers when they use 'conventional signs' to add richness to their own main variables of latitude, longitude and height above sea-level. They use symbols to denote houses, trees, churches, youth hostels, post offices and so on.

Similarly, I use a large number of extra variables in order to be as clear as possible. They include those shown in Table 1.2.

Table 1.2 Some extra variables

Anxiety
Obsessions
Compulsions
Phobias
Irritability
Hallucinations
Delusions
Pain
Disorientation
Anger

Table 1.2 Continued

Fear
Guilt
Repugnance
Boredom
Depersonalization
Derealization
and so on

These extra variables assume particular importance in Chapter 6, when plotting mental illnesses.

1.3 Special variables

A third kind of variable will be discussed in Chapter 2. These are the special variables, as listed in Table 1.3.

Table 1.3 Special variables

Attachment
Attachment breached (as in the 'outsider')
Enlightenment

These are much discussed in religious and mystical literature but remain very elusive. I merely provide, in Chapter 2, a notation for representing them.

1.4 Chapter summary

The term 'ordinary life' covers a wide range of mental states. The main variables of the *map* are as follows.

Mind work
This is equivalent to 'general arousal'. We notice it when it differs from the 'average' level.

General mood, intensity and aspects of mind
Mood is either pleasant or unpleasant. Unselfconscious average states of ordinary life are pleasant. A set of 'aspects of mind' go up or down with the intensity of general mood and

change from pleasant to unpleasant, or vice versa, with it. These aspects of mind are expressed by the mystics as: Knowledge, Unity and Eternity; Light and Body sense; Joy; and Freedom.

On-line and off-line functions

When we exchange information or energy with our environment we are 'on-line'. We go 'off-line' to daydream vaguely, or to think hard or fantasize. The skills for 'on-line' behaviour are stored and ready for use. Separate memories of them are not always retained after their ordinary performance.

Sleeping and waking

We often forget our dreams. We have periods of rapid eye movements (REM) during which we have vivid dreams. Dreams vary in general mood and in mind work. Dream logic can be very different from everyday logic. We remain sufficiently on-line during sleep to monitor our environment.

Attention and things

Attention is like a mental currency. We 'pay' attention to things.

Concentration of attention

We concentrate our attention when we want to observe something more carefully. When overwhelmed by things we become muddled and have to concentrate more, or do more mind work, to restore our 'grip'.

Diffusion of attention

When attention is low, in comparison with the number of things to which it is being paid, it is being diffused as opposed to concentrated.

Extra variables, such as anxiety, obsessions and compulsions must be added in order to portray the subtle variety of mental life, especially in mental illnesses.

Special variables are listed and will be discussed later.

Chapter 2

Mysticism

The word 'mysticism' refers to the experiences and behaviour of the people who are called, in general, 'mystics'. There are mystical traditions within most, if not all, religions and, in addition, some mystics are agnostics or even atheists. Religions often seem to have been founded by mystics and later to have been periodically revived by them.

The word 'mystic' itself comes from the Greek verb *muein* meaning 'to close', as when closing the eyes or closing the mouth. It was used to describe the pilgrims to Eleusis, where the rites of one of the mysteries took place in the ancient world, because they were forbidden to speak of what they had 'seen' afterwards.

We have now mentioned two of the main aspects of mysticism. It concerns an unusual kind of experience obtained other than by the senses. And it must not – or perhaps it cannot – be described, i.e. it is 'ineffable'.

Within religions, mystical knowledge is usually interpreted as being a direct knowledge of the divine, a direct knowledge of God. By 'direct' is meant other than by way of the senses. Moreover, the experiences of mysticism are so overwhelming that even agnostic or atheist mystics seek for the biggest words in their vocabulary to express them. They talk of Nature, or The Cosmos, or The Absolute.

There is a vast literature on mysticism: about mystical experiences; about the mystical procedures which lead to mystical experiences; and about the various interpretations of mystical experiences. Easy access to this literature is afforded by the books of Happold (1963), Stace (1960), Fremantle (1965), Laski (1961), Underhill (1911) and many others. Some of the mystics, such as Traherne, are poets. Some, like Saint Teresa are enthusiastic in the psychological analysis of their own mental states, and some, like Meister Eckhart, are of dazzling intellect.

Mystical texts, i.e. pieces of writing by mystics, usually mix together descriptions of their mystical experiences with several other components, as shown in Table 2.1

Table 2.1 Components of mystical texts

Mystical components
Mystical experiences
Mystical procedures
Mystical interpretations, in terms of religious or other ideas

Additional components
Theological ⎫
Philosophical ⎬ other than the interpretations mentioned above
Biographical ⎪
Other ⎭

2.1 Analysis of mystical language

On reading mystical texts, various features soon become apparent. My analysis owes much to those of James (1902), Stace (1960), Laski (1961) and Happold (1963).

Content

The content of descriptions of mystical states is very limited. The mystics constantly refer to seven main ideas which are shown in Table 2.2. These are the aspects of mind mentioned in Section 1.1 of Chapter 1.

I have used capital letters to begin these words because the mystics themselves often do so, and indeed they clearly mean that these words should be pronounced with emphasis. They are *Real* Knowledge, *Absolute* Unity, *Complete* Freedom and so on, and are to be clearly distinguished from their non-mystical counterparts which do not deserve an initial capital letter, such as knowledge, i.e. *mere* knowledge or *mere* 'book-learning', unity, eternity and so on.

Table 2.2 Aspects of mind: the seven main ideas in the
content of mystical states

Knowledge
Unity
Eternity
Light
Body sense
Joy
Freedom

Although the above words themselves recur frequently in
the mystical literature, the ideas they express are also conveyed
with the aid of a series of literary devices as shown in Table 2.3

Table 2.3 Literary devices

Synonyms,
Similes,
Metaphors and
Associated ideas which, in turn, can be operated upon by
Double negation
Redundancy
Paradox

In Table 2.4 I have displayed six of the main ideas, the aspects
of mind, and some of their transformations, using these literary devices. It is a fascinating exercise to analyse mystical texts
with them in mind. The device called negation, indicated by a
minus sign, denotes the change from pleasant to unpleasant
state, from 'light' to 'dark'.

The seven main ideas can be related to some of the traditional 'faculties' of the mind, as shown in Table 2.5.

Light can be taken to stand not only for vision, which is most
often mentioned by the mystics, but also for the other 'distance' senses of hearing and smell. B, for Body sense, the sense
of one's own body, can stand for interoception as opposed to
exteroception.

Unity can be explained a little by adding 'belongingness' and
Eternity by the phrase 'eternal now' and even, perhaps, 'being'.

Table 2.4 Literary devices used on six of the seven main ideas

Symbol (X)	Main ideas and associated ideas	Negation (−X)	Double negation (−−X)	Redundancy (XX or X−−X)	Paradox (X−X or −XX)
K	Knowledge reality truth absolute	ignorance illusion falsehood	unveil the truth dispel an illusion	real knowledge absolute reality	learned ignorance
U	Unity perfection infinity completeness	disunity imperfection finiteness boundaries	no boundaries no divisions	complete unity	multiplicity in unity
E	Eternity eternal now	time mortality death	timelessness immortality deathlessness	eternal time-lessness	the timeless moment
L	Light fire sparks rays	darkness shadow ashes	shadowless	brilliant light	dazzling obscurity
J	Joy bliss delight	misery despair	relieved of misery	blissful joy	joyful pain
F	Freedom liberty	bondage servitude	released from bondage	at liberty and free	'…whom to serve is perfect freedom'

Table 2.5 The seven main ideas (aspects of mind) related to some faculties of the mind

	Seven main ideas (aspects of mind)	Faculty
K	Knowledge, significance	
U	Unity, belongingness	Cognition
E	Eternity, eternal now, being	
L	Light, exteroception	
B	Body sense, interoception	Perception
J	Joy	Emotion
F	Freedom	Volition

Note also that Unity can be seen to be representing 'space' and Eternity, its own complement, i.e. 'clock-time'.

In addition to the seven main ideas, above, which continually recur in the mystical literature, each mystic will, of course, introduce other ideas related to his own personality, religion, culture, life story and so on. Nevertheless, it is striking how mystics from all historical periods and cultures should repeatedly emphasize the same few ideas that have been discussed above. It is this narrow selection of ideas that renders a mystical text so recognizable and which allows its message, seemingly, to transcend time and culture.

Comments
In addition to naming the aspects of mind making up the content of their mystical states, and elaborating them by literary devices, the mystics also frequently comment upon their states. Their comments, too, are few in range. The main ones are shown in Table 2.6.

Table 2.6 Comments upon mystical states

Intensity
Certainty
Clarity
Ineffability
Sudden onset
Change of personality

The intense, nay, at times the absolute sense of certainty which the mystics describe, is applied to the cognitive group of the seven main ideas. They feel absolutely Certain that they have discovered the True Meaning of the Universe. They feel completely Sure that they are United with the Cosmos. They know that they inhabit the Timeless realm of the Eternal now.

The clarity they describe is partly a metaphorical clarity, related to their certain Knowledge, and it is partly a reference to the quality of their perception, as if their organs of sight, hearing, smell and taste had been spring-cleaned. The world looks brighter and cleaner to them. The sense of their Body is also affected. They have a feeling of lightness and well-being.

Certainty and clarity do not relate directly to Joy or Freedom, but can be seen to do so indirectly, by way of their effect on cognition and perception. Similarly, Joy and Freedom could be seen to affect each other.

Ineffability, which is a word derived from the Latin verb *fari* ('to speak'), is used to convey the mystics' inability to express their mystical experience. Clearly this ineffability cannot be complete, in view of the vast extent of the mystical literature. Nevertheless the mystics all complain of their difficulty in putting their experience into words, and this difficulty gets more acute as they proceed to the more intense mystical states which will be described later. Section 12.5 of Chapter 12 discusses this important topic, of ineffability, in greater depth.

The sudden onset of mystical states is frequently described. In particular, the change in the clarity of perception may be so sudden that it is like a flash of lightning or a sudden flame. (Following a mystical state there is probably, usually, a slow decline via less intense states, but this is not often mentioned. Some mystical states however go to a limit and beyond it. See later.)

The change of personality that occurs in the mystics is perhaps the most important feature of mysticism. It is this change which makes some mystics into such effective pioneers. They seem to acquire abundant energy and confidence. They may also become somewhat unpredictable, and this may be related to a change in their motivation. They no longer seem attached to 'worldly' values. Some are described as Holy Fools.

2.2 Mystical experiences

Although the term 'mystical state' is often used as if to imply
that there is only one such state, in fact mystical experiences
form a large family. It may be that the various types of mystical
state merge into each other by small degrees. However, for
ease of description I shall consider some typical examples of
these states, and then talk about them and place them on
diagrams and maps as if they were discrete.

Mystical State Proper

I use the term 'Mystical State Proper' to denote a fully-
developed mystical state, but one which is not so intense as to
have become completely ineffable, i.e. completely indescrib-
able. I also use this term to distinguish such fully-developed
mystical states from less intense mystical states, for which I
have borrowed Maslow's (1968) term, 'Peak Experiences'.

I think that Mystical States Proper are described by the
mystics using rather abstract words. They often seem to use the
seven main ideas in their unadorned, unelaborated form. They
actually talk about Unity, Eternity and so on. Moreover they
also express these ideas with great intensity.

The following passage, by R. M. Bucke, illustrates these
qualities, those of the Mystical State Proper.

> I had spent the evening in a great city, with two friends
> reading and discussing poetry and philosophy. We parted
> at midnight. I had a long drive to my lodging. My mind,
> deeply under the influence of the ideas, images and
> emotions called up by the reading and talk, was calm and
> peaceful. I was in a state of quiet, even passive enjoyment,
> not actually thinking, but letting ideas, images and
> emotions flow of themselves, as it were, through my mind.
> All at once, without warning of any kind, I found myself
> wrapped in a flame-coloured cloud. For an instant I
> thought of fire, an immense conflagration somewhere close
> by in that great city; the next instant I knew that that fire
> was in myself. Directly afterwards there came upon me a
> sense of exultation, of immense joyousness, accompanied
> or immediately followed by an intellectual illumination
> quite impossible to describe. Among other things, I did not

merely come to believe, I saw that the universe is not composed of dead matter, but is, on the contrary, a living Presence; I became conscious in myself of eternal life. It was not a conviction that I would have eternal life, but a consciousness that I possessed eternal life then; I saw that all men are immortal; that the cosmic order is such that without any peradventure all things work together for the good of each and all.

Bucke was a Canadian psychiatrist. The passage above is quoted by William James in his chapter on mysticism in *The Varieties of Religious Experience* (1902). It is also quoted in Happold (1963).

Peak Experience
Here, in the next text, is a famous passage from Thomas Traherne (quoted in Happold, 1963) who was a seventeenth-century English clergyman.

The corn was orient and immortal wheat, which never should be reaped, nor was ever sown. I thought it had stood from everlasting to everlasting. The dust and stones of the street were as precious as gold: the gates were at first the end of the world. The green trees when I saw them first through one of the gates transported and ravished me, their sweetness and unusual beauty made my heart to leap, and almost mad with ecstasy, they were such strange and wonderful things. The men! O what venerable and reverend creatures did the aged seem! Immortal Cherubims! And young men glittering and sparkling Angels, and maids strange seraphic pieces of life and beauty! Boys and girls tumbling in the street, and playing, were moving jewels. I knew not that they were born or should die; But all things abided eternally as they were in their proper places. Eternity was manifest in the Light of the Day, and something infinite behind everything appeared: which talked with my expectation and moved my desire. The city seemed to stand in Eden, or to be built in Heaven. The streets were mine, the temple was mine, the people were mine, their clothes and gold and silver were mine, as much as their sparkling eyes, fair skins, and ruddy faces. The skies were mine, and so were the sun and moon and stars, and all the World was mine; and I the only spectator and enjoyer of it. I knew no churlish proprieties, nor bounds, nor divisions: but all proprieties and divisions were mine: all treasures and the possessors of them. So that with much ado I was corrupted, and made to learn the dirty devices of this world. Which now I unlearn, and become, as it were, a little child again that I may enter into the Kingdom of God.

It seems to me that this passage is *slightly* less intense than that of Bucke and that it contains more ideas. It *does* contain some big abstract ideas but in addition it mentions a lot of specific things – trees, gates, jewels and so on. It reminds me of the glowing paintings of Samuel Palmer.

I think that Peak Experiences are sometimes in the Border Zone between ordinary life and mystical states. If the Intensity drops even further I think one gets to the Average State, in which we spend much of our time in ordinary life. What is more, I think that the transitions between the three states just mentioned are all reversible, as shown thus:

Average   ⇄   Peak   ⇄   Mystical
State   Experience   State Proper

Peak Experiences sometimes occur to people spontaneously, especially under the influence of aesthetic or emotional experiences such as absorption in nature, sexual attraction, the intellectual excitement of scientific discovery, or philosophical or mathematical insight. Marghanita Laski (1961) has described these various 'triggers'. However, I also think Peak Experiences can be deliberately attained by the practice of mystical procedures. They are then seen as an early stage along the mystical path, to be followed, in due course, by the more intense Mystical States Proper. Progress along the mystical path is probably like going up a few steps and then down a few, gradually rising up the stairs.

One description of a 'trigger', in fiction, is that of Gudrun seeing Gerald, in the first chapter of *Women in Love* by D. H. Lawrence (1921). Another is where Harry Haller, the 'Wolf of the Steppes', becomes elated when he takes part in a masked ball (Hesse, 1927). Yet another is where a scientist makes a discovery, in *The Search* by C. P. Snow (1934).

The Void

When the mystics follow the mystical path to its limit they reach a place where intensity seems also to reach its limit, and where all the seven main ideas become maximal. At this place ineffability also becomes maximal, so that the mystics all say that nothing at all can be said about this state. (I shall discuss these strange statements in theoretical terms later.) In spite of this total ineffability the Islamic mystic al-Ghazali (quoted in Happold, 1963) makes a brave attempt to describe the inde-scribable, as follows:

> Now, when this state prevails, it is called in relation to him who experiences it, Extinction, nay Extinction of Extinction, for the soul has become extinct to itself, extinct to its own extinction, for it becomes unconscious of itself and unconscious of its own unconsciousness, since were it conscious of its own unconsciousness, it would be conscious of itself.

The Void is not so much a place, in the sense that the Peak Experience and the Mystical State Proper are places at which a mystic can spend some time, but a point of sudden transition (this will be expressed later, in Chapter 3, Section 3.2, *The geometry of the* map). Another name for The Void is *Nirvana*, which means the process of being blown out, as a candle flame is blown out. This expresses the idea that The Void is not so much a place as a process, a change of state (this distinction between place and process is also important at other places on the *map*). I can now extend my network of states:

Average ⇄ Peak ⇄ Mystical → The
State   Experience State Proper Void

Note, however, that the arrow indicating the transition from the Mystical State Proper to The Void goes in a single direc-tion. The mystical literature emphasises that from the Mystical State Proper the mystical path goes through a 'point of no return'. From here the mystic must pass on and through The

Void in order to return, as we shall see, to where he started (or to a place that is nearly the same as where he started).

The Dark Mystical State Proper

Now we must study another set of members of the family of mystical states, but a set which is 'Dark' in quality. The Dark equivalent of the Mystical State Proper is sometimes called the 'dark night of the soul'. Here, then, is a passage by St John of the Cross who used this phrase (quoted by Stace, 1960). (St John was a sixteenth-century Spanish monk and the spiritual director of St Teresa of Ávila.)

> But what the sorrowing soul feels most painfully in this condition is the dreadful thought that God has abandoned it and has flung it into utter darkness . . . it feels most vividly the shadows and laments of death and the torments of hell which consist in the conviction that God in his anger has chastized and forsaken it for ever.

Notice how the aspects of the mind are reversed, to their Dark versions, while still leaving a great intensity. The Dark states are on the unpleasant side of the *map*, in the unpleasant general mood. The dark side of the network is as follows.

Dark	$\rightleftarrows$ Dark Peak	$\rightleftarrows$ Dark Mystical	$\rightarrow$ The
Average State	Experience	State Proper	Void

Dark Peak Experiences

For an example of a Dark Peak Experience I have chosen a passage by Charles Marshall (in Fremantle, 1965), a seventeenth-century Quaker, who suffered for his faith.

> I spent much time in retirements alone, in the fields and woods, and by springs of water, which I delighted to lie by and drink of. And in those days of retirement, strong, great, and many were my cries unto the Lord; and sometimes being retired into places free from passengers, to ease my heart, I did cry aloud, because of disquietness of spirit. And I had openings of the miserable fall and inexpressible degeneration of mankind, and the captivity and bondage which my soul lay in; in the sense of which state of bondage and thraldom, I cried out. Oh, that my

soul might be eased from these heavy burdens and loads of death and darkness! that out of this state of gross Egyptian darkness I might be saved, and from the land of drought, a land of anguish, a land of horrible darkness! Oh, undeclarable fall! said my soul; oh, inexpressible wall of partition and separation! Oh, gulf unutterable! For the fallen and undone state of the sons and daughters of men was opened unto me, beyond all words to demonstrate.

Like Traherne he expresses a lot of ideas, including some of the big, abstract ones, but they are all now on the Dark side. The intensity seems to me to be slightly lower than in the passage by St John of the Cross.

I think that Dark Average States belong, as do Average States, to ordinary life. I mean by Dark Average States those states in which we feel generally 'out-of-sorts', have a 'malaise', or the feeling that things are not going too well. A bad hangover may perhaps be a typical example of a Dark Average State. There are Border Zones between Average States and Peak Experiences, and between Dark Average States and Dark Peak Experiences.

I can now extend my network of states yet again but, like an early terrestrial cartographer, I shall have to leave parts of the map blank, for this is indeed one of the preliminary sketches for my detailed *map*. I have drawn the Dark series of states symmetrical to the others, and have put a single arrow to The Void from the Dark Mystical State Proper although I am not sure about this direct route. See Figure 2.1.

Different traditions vary in the emphasis they place on the Dark states. St John of the Cross regards them as essential whereas the Buddha mentions them (Nyanatiloka, 1950) without particular emphasis as merely hindrances to be overcome.

The mystical path leads back to the Average State (and, perhaps, also, back to the Dark Average State) so I have got to complete the two circles. I do so by way of two other states which I shall label with question marks and which I will discuss later (see Figure 2.1). (Other states will also be added, later.)

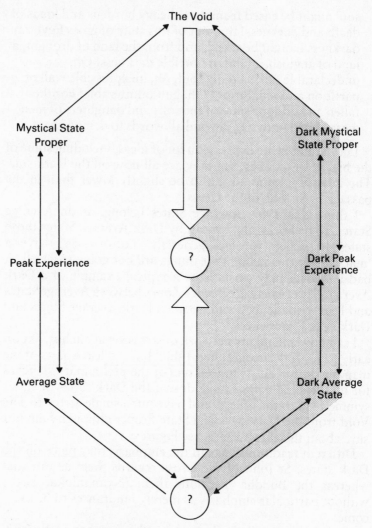

Figure 2.1 Network of states.
Two states to be named later

2.3 Mystical procedures

Although Peak Experiences sometimes occur spontaneously,
the systematic passage around the mystical path requires one
or more deliberate 'mystical procedures' to be used with great

persistence. The most important of these seems to be meditation. There are also various ancillary procedures.

Apart from these there is also, usually, what I call an 'orientation procedure' which involves a deliberate setting out upon the mystical path. It requires the novice to follow various rules of behaviour, to read certain books, associate with certain people or study under certain teachers. These various mystical procedures are listed in Table 2.7.

Table 2.7 Mystical procedures

1 Orientation	Following certain rules of behaviour
	Associating with particular people
	Reading selected books
	Studying under certain teachers
2 Meditation	Raja Yoga, e.g. of Patanjali
	Buddhist meditation including Zazen
	The Prayer of Jesus
	and so on
3 Ancillary	
	Physically active, such as dancing, singing, or snake-handling
	Physically passive, such as solitude, sleep deprivation and
	exposure to hot, cold and wet weather; or
	taking a drug such as peyote

Meditation is the key method and it is found in all the main traditions. Patanjali's *Yoga Aphorisms* (Stephen, 1957) contain a clear description of meditation. I have devised a rather free version of Patanjali's method (Clark, 1970) in the form of a flow diagram (Figure 2.2).

Meditation is a method by which a person concentrates more and more upon less and less. The aim is to empty the mind while, paradoxically, remaining alert. Normally, if we empty our minds, as we do when we settle down to sleep – for instance, 'counting sheep' to narrow our thoughts – we become lethargic and eventually go to sleep. The paradox of meditation is that it both empties the mind and, at the same time, encourages alertness.

The flow diagram, shown in Figure 2.2, emphasizes the step-by-step nature of meditation. The various sub-procedures are arranged from simple ones like posture, hearing, breathing

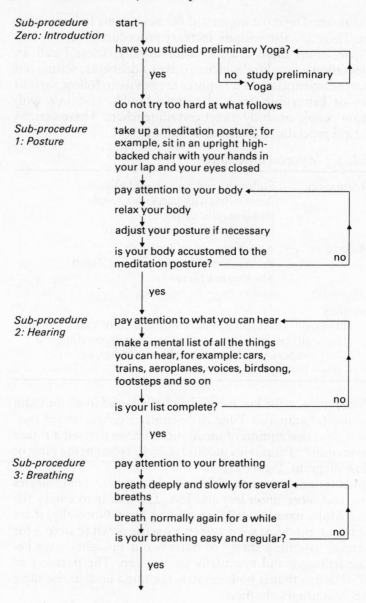

Sub-procedure Zero: Introduction

start

have you studied preliminary Yoga?

yes — no → study preliminary Yoga

do not try too hard at what follows

Sub-procedure 1: Posture

take up a meditation posture; for example, sit in an upright high-backed chair with your hands in your lap and your eyes closed

pay attention to your body

relax your body

adjust your posture if necessary

is your body accustomed to the meditation posture? — no

yes

Sub-procedure 2: Hearing

pay attention to what you can hear

make a mental list of all the things you can hear, for example: cars, trains, aeroplanes, voices, birdsong, footsteps and so on

is your list complete? — no

yes

Sub-procedure 3: Breathing

pay attention to your breathing

breath deeply and slowly for several breaths

breath normally again for a while

is your breathing easy and regular? — no

yes

Figure 2.2 Flow diagram of Patanjali's Yoga meditation procedure

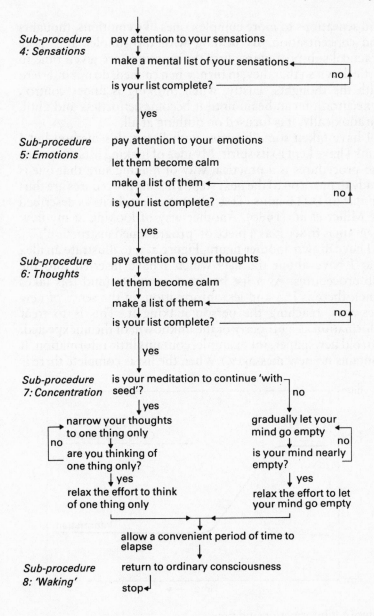

Sub-procedure 4: Sensations
pay attention to your sensations
make a mental list of your sensations
is your list complete? — no
yes

Sub-procedure 5: Emotions
pay attention to your emotions
let them become calm
make a list of them
is your list complete? — no
yes

Sub-procedure 6: Thoughts
pay attention to your thoughts
let them become calm
make a list of them
is your list complete? — no
yes

Sub-procedure 7: Concentration
is your meditation to continue 'with seed'?
yes / no

narrow your thoughts to one thing only
are you thinking of one thing only?
no
yes
relax the effort to think of one thing only

gradually let your mind go empty
is your mind nearly empty?
no
yes
relax the effort to let your mind go empty

allow a convenient period of time to elapse

Sub-procedure 8: 'Waking'
return to ordinary consciousness
stop

and sensations to more complex ones like emotions, thoughts and concentration. By dealing with the simpler and more practical sub-procedures first the emotions are given time to settle down so that they, in turn, when calmed, do not interfere with the thoughts. Lastly, when thinking is under control, concentration can begin until it becomes effortless and until, paradoxically, it is focused on nothing at all.

I have taken some liberties with Patanjali's method but I think I have kept to its spirit. My idea of making lists at various sub-procedures is a practical way of making sure that one is ready to move on to the next step. The sub-procedures are thus similar to TOTE units (Test, Operate, Test, Exit) as described by Miller *et al.* (1960). Another way of looking at my flow diagram is to see it as a piece of 'programmed instruction'.

I have drawn another figure, Figure 2.3, to illustrate an idea that I have about the lists which I have inserted into the sub-procedures. As a list becomes complete (and this takes time), there is less and less information, in the sense of new messages, reaching the person making it. This is to treat information as a property of the unknown, of the unexpected. (An old newspaper, for example, contains little information. It contains no new messages.) When the list is complete there is

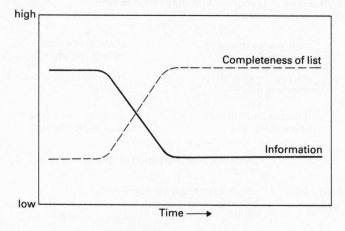

Figure 2.3 Information and time.
Information being reduced with the passage of time, during sub-procedures of Yoga meditation

no more information, or very little, reaching the person and it is then time to move on to the next sub-procedure.

If a person meditates regularly he may eventually start to move along the mystical path towards Peak Experiences and beyond. However, the mystical path is not a straightforward highway. A person may become too euphoric until his state is, perhaps, indistinguishable from hypomania (a less severe version of the mental illness called mania). He is then likely to become overfull of his own importance – in other words to become conceited. He is also likely to become excited and he may then become confused and even hallucinated. We are here in another Border Zone. Among the mystics there are a number of 'visionaries', such as William Blake, whose writings, though fascinating, are complex and far from easy to understand (Blake, c.1808). Even the classic mystics, such as St Teresa of Ávila, occasionally had visions and auditions, i.e. heard voices, but it is characteristic of these traditional mystics that they do not regard visions and auditions as important, and that they are, in fact, suspicious of them.

Another pitfall of the mystical path is for the mystic to find himself on the Dark side, suffering from Dark Peak Experiences or Dark Mystical States Proper. The mystics are then advised by their spiritual directors or *gurus* to 'press on', with the assurance that both sides of the mystical path eventually lead to The Void, beyond.

2.4 Special variables: a notation for attachment and enlightenment

I find the following symbolism convenient but I do not claim that it explains anything in itself. Attachment and enlightenment remain deeply elusive in spite of everything that has been written about them.

Attachment

If a person is at a particular state of mind, X, I express his becoming attached by placing a line on either side of the X, thus:

$$X \rightleftarrows |X|$$

This symbol, $|X|$, represents the attached person being cut off or hidden, by some kind of barrier, from his true self which is shown, without attachment, by the symbol **X**. The symbol $|X|$ seems to fit many of the metaphors which are used to describe attachment. I show the process of attachment as being reversible by using two arrows. The *Bhagavad-Gita* contains a lengthy explanation of attachment. Several varieties of it are also encountered by *The Little Prince* in the book by Saint-Exupéry (1945).

The outsider
When an attached person becomes aware of his attachment and seeks to get rid of it, I show him as almost literally 'seeing through it', thus:

$$X \rightleftarrows |X| \rightleftarrows |X|$$

The lines are now broken. This corresponds to the state of the 'outsider' (Wilson, 1956; Camus, 1942), the person who sees through attachment, who is disillusioned, and who may now feel anxious and insecure, as shown thus:

$$X \rightleftarrows |X| \rightleftarrows |X| \text{ with anxiety}$$

This state of being an anxious outsider is often described as an early step along the mystical path. It corresponds, roughly, to the possession of the 'sick soul' described by William James (1902).

Enlightenment
For the enlightened person I use an asterisk. This reminds me of the twinkle in the eye, albeit a rather ferocious twinkle, seen in pictures of Zen masters. I call **A***, A–star.

Enlightenment is usually described as a state which follows when a person makes one or more cycles of the mystical path. I can now represent this as in Figure 2.4.

I have given names to the two states marked with question marks in Figure 2.1. The Origin, **O**, is so-named partly because it will be seen later to be at the geometrical origin of my *map*. The Zero State, **Z**, can be regarded as a doorway in and out of the Origin. The hollow arrows indicate instantaneous changes in mind work without any change in the other variables. Note that the arrow from **V** to **O** is one-way.

2.5 Stages on the mystical path

Different mystics use different terms for the stages along the mystical path and so I have tried to produce a set of standard terms which refer to the network of mental states. Here is my tentative list of terms, set out in Table 2.8, and used in Table 2.9 to compare three authors.

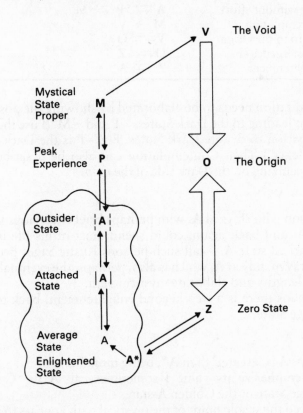

Figure 2.4 Enlightenment.
Different versions of the **A**-state are grouped together.

Table 2.8 The stages on the mystical path (omitting Dark states)

Stage	Symbol
1 Attachment	$A \rightleftarrows |A|$
2 Disillusionment	$|A| \rightleftarrows |A|$
3 Orientation	$|A| \rightleftarrows |A|$ with a new goal
4 Concentration	$|A| \rightleftarrows |A|$ with concentration
5 Meditation	
(i) with effort	$|A| \rightleftarrows P$ with concentration
(ii) without effort	$|A| \rightleftarrows P \rightleftarrows M$
6 Contemplation	$M \rightarrow V$
7 Return to the Origin	$V \Longrightarrow O$
8 Re-emergence	$O \Longleftarrow Z$
9 Enlightenment	$Z \rightleftarrows A^*$

Meditation needs to be elaborated by showing the possibility of it leading to the Dark States, $-P$ and $-M$. (I use the sign of negation to denote Dark States. E.g. $-P$ is the Dark Peak Experience.) Then Contemplation can also be described as also occurring on the Dark side of the *map*.

$$-M \rightarrow V$$

A person who stays at **A**, with perhaps brief excursions to $|A|$ and $|A|$ and back again, could spend most of his life in the unattached state **A**. I call such persons Rustic Sages because they stay mainly at **A**, which is also, perhaps, the eventual goal of the lengthy and elaborate mystical path.

Perhaps there is a step beyond enlightenment, back to the Average State?

$$A^* \rightarrow A$$

Perhaps **A** is 'greater' than A^*, being more human?

To emphasize its value I sometimes call **A** the Golden Average State or the Golden A-state.

Indeed the whole point of the mystical path appears to be to help people back to **A**, back to being human again. It helps people to 'become what they are'. Enlightened people can tell where a person is on the mystical path because they have been along it themselves. (Rustic Sages probably cannot.)

If I am right about Rustic Sages it would appear that the mystical path is not essential. There are many remarks to that effect in the Zen Buddhist tradition. 'Everyday life is Zen' they say, and 'Walk on!' (see Blythe, 1942). It also seems to be the main teaching of that arch anti-*guru*, Krishnamurti (Lutyens, 1970).

Many other authors can be analysed in a similar way; for example St John of the Cross (in Happold, 1963), Patanjali (Stephen, 1957) and the author of the *Bhagavad-Gita* (Prabhavananda and Isherwood, 1947).

Some authors, such as St Teresa, use different metaphors in different books in their attempts to convey some of the stages.

One very important metaphor is that of 'death', despair and 'rebirth', as explored widely by Doel (1973). Attachment is seen as 'death', that is to say 'spiritual death'. Disillusionment follows, i.e. the stage of despair. Orientation offers hope, and the journey along the mystical path ends in 'rebirth'.

Another important metaphor is that of the Garden of Eden and the Fall.

This brief discussion of metaphors has led us into the heart of the theological approach to mysticism which weaves mystical experiences into the particular theological tradition. The feelings of intense certainty that occur in mystical states are then transferred to the beliefs of that particular tradition.

2.6 The unitive life

The last stage of the mystical path, when the mystic returns, transformed, enlightened, to the 'market-place', to ordinary life, gives rise to several different types of description. William James (1902) discusses it mainly in the context of Christian 'saintliness'. Evelyn Underhill (1911) emphasizes the sheer vitality of this stage, its abundance of energy, and even its gaiety, as typified by St Teresa of Ávila writing little songs for her novices. These are the qualities that make some of the mystics into pioneers – practical people who reform religious orders or start new ones or galvanize a nation to defend itself.

Other authors point to another quality of this stage, the quality of unexpectedness, of surprise, of jokiness. This is the quality of the Zen master as he teases his pupils with the enigmas called *koans* (Reps, 1957). Pushed further – beyond a

Table 2.9 The mystical path described by three authors

	Richard of St Victor *(in Happold, 1963)*	St Teresa of Ávila *(in Happold, 1963)*	The Ten Bulls *by Kakuan (in Reps, 1957)*
1 Attachment			
2 Disillusionment			1. Search for the Bull
3 Orientation	First degree (of passionate charity)	First degree (or stage) of prayer	2. Discovering the foot prints
			3. Perceiving the Bull
4 Concentration			4. Catching the Bull
5 Meditation			
(i) with effort	Second degree	Second degree	5. Taming the Bull
(ii) without effort			6. Riding the Bull home
6 Contemplation		Third degree (prayer of quiet)	7. The Bull transcended
7 Return to the origin	Third degree	Fourth degree	8. Both Bull and self transcended
8 Re-emergence	Fourth degree		9. Reaching the source
9 Enlightenment			10. In the world

human degree – and this unexpected quality becomes the anarchic behaviour of the Trickster figure, the Clown or Fool of the North American Indians (Radin, 1956; Boston, 1974), whose allegiance to the Great Way is so profound that he neglects to protect himself from his own excesses. See also the character named Sunday in *The Man Who Was Thursday*, by G. K. Chesterton (1908).

Other mystics, and perhaps they typify the majority, are described as continuing to live what look like very ordinary lives, quiet and happy (Chandler, 1908). I like to think that their obvious enlightenment gradually fades, leaving behind only an occasional twinkle in the eye.

This quality is also quite often met with in ordinary people who have learnt deeply from life but who have not, so far as one knows, been mystics. I call the latter Rustic Sages, but probably they should have a less pretentious title. I mean to denote people like Eggerson in *The Confidential Clerk* by T. S. Eliot (1944), and the old Shepherd in *The Winter's Tale* by Shakespeare (1623). I suspect that there are a lot of them about, including those people you see cycling back from their allotments.

$$A \rightleftarrows |A| \rightleftarrows |A| \rightleftarrows M \rightarrow V \Longrightarrow O \Longleftrightarrow Z \rightleftarrows A^* \rightarrow A$$
Mystics

$$A \rightleftarrows |A| \rightleftarrows |A| \rightleftarrows A$$
Rustic Sages

I am not sure how one could tell a Rustic Sage from one of the above 'quiet' mystics. After all, what would you ask them?

2.7 Mystical interpretations

Mystical experiences are interpreted in various ways. The most elaborate interpretations are theological. Mythological interpretations are discussed in Chapter 8.

The mystical path can also be seen not only as referring to a particular person, the mystic, but also as being complementary to creation myths. This is discussed in Section 8.3 of Chapter 8.

In this book I put forward a psychological interpretation which does not, however, claim to exclude the other interpretations. The various interpretations can co-exist. Each is an attempt to make sense of what are an amazing series of experiences, from a particular point of view. Table 12.1 in Chapter 12 tabulates some of these interpretations.

2.8 The problem of mysticism

The main problem can be stated thus. Why should the mystical procedures lead, or sometimes lead, to mystical experiences? Subsidiary problems are why such experiences are interpreted in the way that they are? And why a mystical experience is followed, or sometimes followed, by a change in personality?

   Those who believe in the interpretation that mystical experiences are of a divine origin have no difficulty with the above problems, but the enquirer who adopts the point of view of scientific agnosticism is left to ponder on them. (See Section 12.6 in Chapter 12; also see Otto, 1917.)

2.9 Chapter summary

The term mysticism is discussed. Mystical literature is broken down into its components. The content of descriptions of mystical states is analysed as consisting of seven main ideas. These are elaborated using literary devices such as double negation. The seven main ideas are related to some faculties of the mind. Mystical literature also contains comments upon mystical states; some of these comments are listed. Texts are quoted giving examples of the main types of mystical state, and networks of states are drawn. Mystical procedures, including meditation, are analysed and a flow diagram of Patanjali's Yoga method is presented. The stages on the mystical path are given a standard terminology which is then used to analyse three authors. The unitive life is discussed and Rustic Sages are compared with the mystics. Finally, the various interpretations of mystical states and the 'problem of mysticism' are mentioned.

PART TWO

The *map*
itself

This Part of the book deals with the *map* of mental states in its latest version. In Chapter 3 I describe the various features, derived from the sources discussed in Part One, with which I want to build the *map*. Then, step by step, I put it together.

Chapter 3

The structure of the *map*

In this chapter I describe the *map* itself in two quite different ways. First, in Section 3.1, I put together the main variables that have been discussed already in Chapters 1 and 2, in order to build up my *map* of mental states, step by step. Then I show how extra variables can be added to the *map* when required.

Second, in Section 3.2, I construct the *map* as a purely geometrical system based on a cone. I then transform this completely abstract system into the *map* by interpreting its variables as mental variables – the same set of main variables that were used earlier in Chapter 1.

3.1 Constructing the *map* from its main variables

I will now start putting the *map* together, using the set of main variables listed in Table 1.1.

General mood, pleasant and unpleasant
The important distinction between a pleasant and an unpleasant general mood can be shown by a circle divided into two semicircles, as in Figure 3.1. The unpleasant side is shown darker than the pleasant side, and the term dark will often be used instead of unpleasant.

Intensity of general mood
I now introduce an intensity variable which can be applied to either general mood. I show this variable as an angular dimension which runs around both sides of the circle of general mood, as shown in Figure 3.2. The centre of the circle is marked O, for Origin. The large angle, marked with two

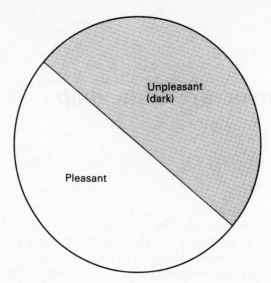

Figure 3.1 General mood, pleasant or unpleasant (dark)

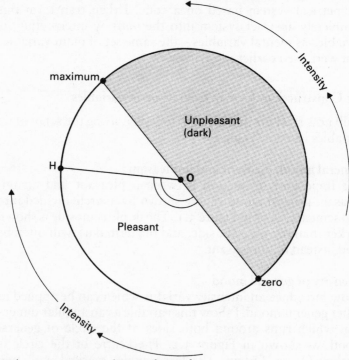

Figure 3.2 Intensity of general mood

curved lines, represents a high intensity of pleasant mood, at a point H. The intensity variable runs from zero to maximum around the semicircles of both the pleasant and the unpleasant general moods.

Average intensity

Next, I introduce the idea of an average amount of intensity, such as I think we experience for much of the time in ordinary life. I place it at the mid-point of the semicircle on each side. I label these two points 'average' (see Figure 3.3). When reading the expression 'average' on the dark side I say 'dark average' or 'unpleasant average'.

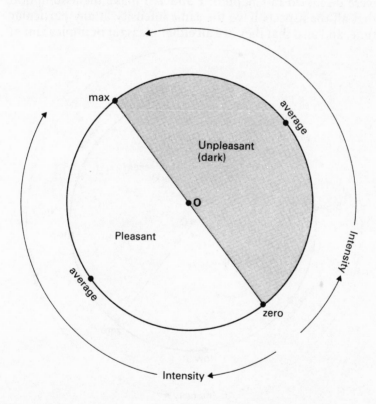

Figure 3.3 Average intensity and dark average intensity of general mood

Low and high intensity
Let me now put in two other amounts of intensity, low and high, on both sides, as shown in Figure 3.4. These points are placed mid-way between the average points and the extreme points on the intensity dimension, zero and maximum (the latter having been abbreviated to max). It is convenient to label such points in this way but, as with the average points, their placing is somewhat arbitrary.

Aspects of mind and intensity
At this stage in the construction of the *map* I need to relate the idea of intensity of general mood to the aspects of mind that were discussed in Chapters 1 and 2. I make the assumption that all the aspects have the same intensity at any particular time, and also that they are all either pleasant or unpleasant at

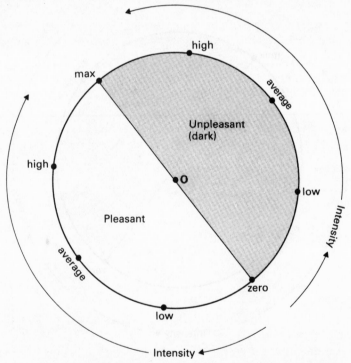

Figure 3.4 Low, high, dark low and dark high intensities, added to average and dark average intensities, of general mood

any particular time. For example, if the general mood is pleasant and the intensity is high, then I assume that all the aspects, as shown in Table 3.1, are experienced as highly pleasant, as in a Peak Experience.

Table 3.1 Pleasant aspects of mind

		Abbreviation
Cognition	Knowledge (meaningfulness, significance)	K
	Unity (belongingness)	U
	Eternity (timelessness)	E
Perception	Light	L
	Body sense	B
Emotion	Joy	J
Volition	Freedom	F

On the other hand, if the general mood is unpleasant and the intensity is still high, I assume the dark or unpleasant aspects shown in Table 3.2 are all experienced, as in a Dark Mystical State.

Table 3.2 Unpleasant or Dark aspects of mind

		Abbreviation
Cognition	Ignorance (meaninglessness, lack of significance)	−K
	Disunity (no belongingness)	−U
	Time (pressing, useless)	−E
Perception	Darkness	−L
	Body sense (uncomfortable, heavy)	−B
Emotion	Misery	−J
Volition	Bondage (loss of Freedom)	−F

Similarly, I take it that, if intensity varies, then all the aspects of the mind vary together. They go up or down together, as intensity goes up or down, whether the general mood is pleasant or unpleasant.

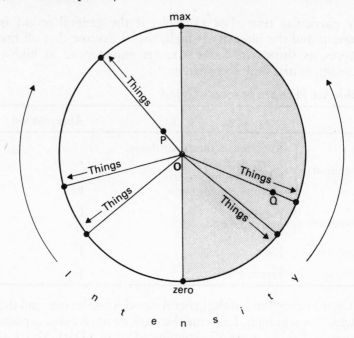

Figure 3.5 Things

Things

I now want to introduce the variable things, that is to say the number of things on the mind at a particular time. To do so I label the radius of the circle 'things', as in Figure 3.5.

Two points, P and Q, have been labelled in Figure 3.5. Starting at O, the origin, the distance to Q is greater than the distance to P, each along a radius. This difference means that there are more things at Q than at P.

We are now able to specify the following by indicating a particular point: the number of things; the degree of intensity; and whether the general mood is pleasant or unpleasant at that point.

Attention units

Next, I need to represent attention units. To do this, I draw a line vertically upwards from the Origin O, as in Figure 3.6.

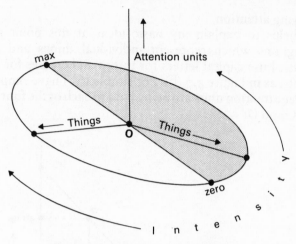

Figure 3.6 Attention units added

We will soon be able to plot a point which represents a particular number of things and the particular number of attention units which are being paid to them. As a first step I detach the things dimension and the attention units dimension from the circle of general mood for a while, as in Figure 3.7 (a). The things and attention units at a point P can now be seen.

Rule 1

I now want to introduce a simple rule, in the form of an equation, as follows:

Rule 1: things + attention units = a parameter

(By parameter I mean a variable whose values can be held constant at particular levels.)

The justification of this rule is that it leads to an extremely simple *map*. Until it becomes clear that a more complicated equation is better, I prefer to stick to this simple one. This seems to be an extension of Occam's Razor: not only is it better to keep 'entities' as few as possible, but also the rules, logical or mathematical, linking the entities should be kept as simple as possible.

Note that Rule 1 depends on an assumption that things and attention units can be added.

Paying attention
It helps to explain my basic ideas at this point if I draw diagrams which represent individual things and attention units. I use capital letters for things and crosses for attention units, as in Figure 3.7 (b). For simplicity, I have supposed that three attention units are being paid to each of the four things A, B, C and D.

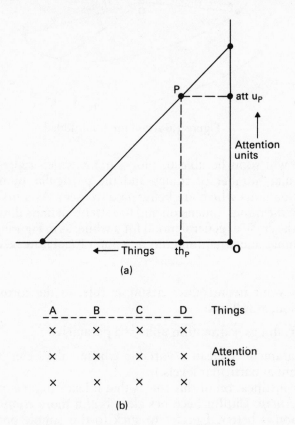

(a)

	A	B	C	D	Things
	×	×	×	×	
	×	×	×	×	Attention units
	×	×	×	×	

(b)

Figure 3.7 Things and attention units
  (a) The co-ordinates of a point P on the two dimensions, things and attention units
  (b) Individual attention units being paid to individual things

Mind work

Now, I am going to take another big step. I am going to call the parameter in Rule 1 mind work. This is the only new term that I have coined for this book. It is formed by analogy with the familiar term brain work, and is its mental equivalent. By mind work I mean a person's degree of alertness or lethargy. Looked at physiologically, I relate mind work to the idea of 'general arousal' (Berlyne, 1969) or just 'arousal' (Wingfield and Byrnes, 1981). Now I can rewrite Rule 1, as follows:

Rule 1A: things + attention units = mind work

It follows from Rule 1A that, for any particular value of mind work, when things are zero then the attention units are equal to mind work. Conversely, if attention units are zero, then the number of things are equal to mind work. These two limiting cases are shown in Figure 3.8.

In other words, when things are zero, the distance between the Origin O and the point P is the number of attention units which are equal to the value of mind work. A similar argument

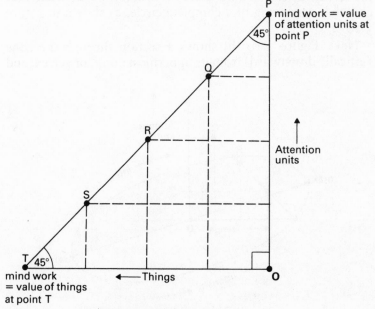

Figure 3.8 Two limiting cases

applies to point T. The line between P and T in Figure 3.8 is a line on which any points such as P, Q, R, S and T are such that the sum of their things co-ordinate and their attention units co-ordinate comes to the same amount, and that amount is the value of mind work.

The triangle TOP is a right-angled triangle and its shorter sides, OT and OP, are equal. The two small angles are both 45° because it is an isosceles triangle and because the angles of any triangle add up to 180°. It may help to draw a triangle like TOP and then measure the things and attention units co-ordinates for any points along PT. It will then be found that the sum of these two distances will always be the same for the particular size of triangle that has been drawn.

We can now put this triangle back into the circle of general mood, as in Figure 3.9. The circle of general mood is seen at an angle and consequently appears elliptical.

The cone
Now we can generate a cone by rotating the triangle around the vertical attention units dimension, as if it were a triangular gate that can swing in a complete circle, as shown in Figure 3.10 (a).

Next, Figure 3.10 (b) shows a section through the cone vertically downwards from its uppermost point, or vertex, and

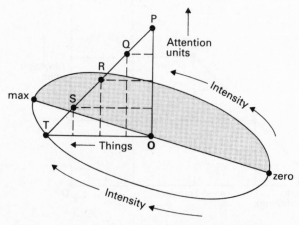

Figure 3.9 The triangle in the circle of general mood

we see that the angle between the sides of the cone, at the vertex, is a right angle. Note that the height, *h*, of the cone is equal to the radius, *r*, because *h* and *r* are sides of isosceles triangles. (Please note that although some Figures show taller cones, the *map* requires a right-angled one.)

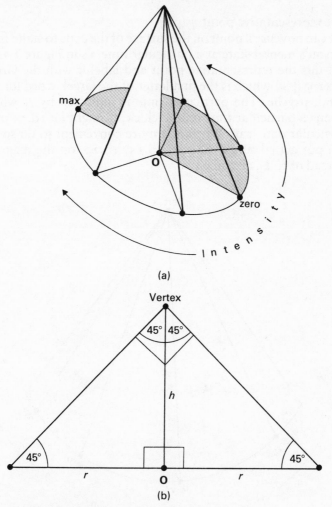

Figure 3.10 Generating a cone
      (a) Swinging the triangular 'gate' in a complete circle
      (b) A right angle at the Vertex of the cone

Now we can make part of the surface of the cone opaque by shading half of the cone, the half which is vertically above the unpleasant half of the circle of general mood. The circle of general mood now forms the base of the cone, as shown in Figure 3.11.

The representative point ψ (psi)

We can now use a point on the surface of the cone to stand for a person's mental state at a particular time, as in Figure 3.12. I call this the representative point and label it with the Greek letter ψ (psi) which is the first letter of the Greek word for the mind, psyche. The particular time is indicated by t_1 which means a particular time on the clock. It might be 10.15 on a particular date, say. When it is more convenient to do so we can put actual times, such as 10.15, 10.20, on the diagram instead of t_1, t_2, and so on.

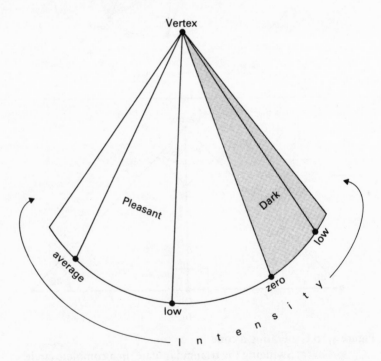

Figure 3.11 The unpleasant or dark half of the cone, shown shaded

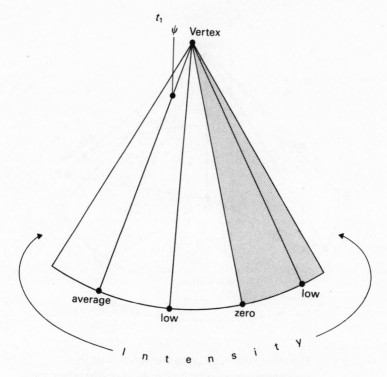

Figure 3.12 The representative point ψ (psi)

If we make the surface of the cone transparent again we can see that the representative point shows: the person's intensity of general mood; whether the general mood is pleasant or unpleasant; the amount of things and of attention units; and, if we look at the height (or the radius) of the cone, the value of mind work. All these variables are shown at a particular time in Figure 3.13, in this case t_1. Note, again, that the height of the cone h always equals the radius r, because the angle at the vertex of this cone is a right angle. It follows that four angles are 45°, as shown in Figure 3.10 (b). Hence the triangles are isosceles and therefore $h = r$.

Different levels of mind work
By varying the height h of the cone (or its radius r) we can represent varying levels of the parameter, mind work. A very

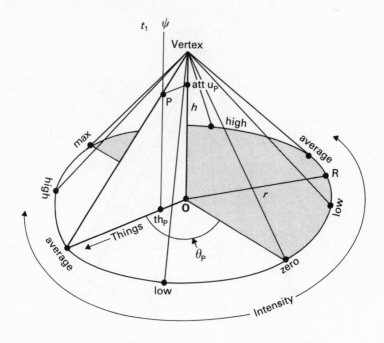

Figure 3.13 The information given by the position of the
representative point ψ (psi) at P (given that the cone is
right-angled: h = height of the cone from Origin, O, to
Vertex; r = radius of the cone from O to R; $h = r$; th_P
= things co-ordinate of P; att u_P = attention units
co-ordinate of P; θ_P = angular co-ordinate of P)

large cone will then represent an excited state with a very high
level of mind work, and a very small cone will represent a very
lethargic state. In between will be cones of average size,
representing an average level of mind work, as shown in Figure
3.14.

Figure 3.14 (a) is a section through three cones, shown
nested within each other. They are then shown as complete
cones at (b), with high, average and low levels of mind work, at
different times. (Appendix II includes designs for making a
model of such a cone.)

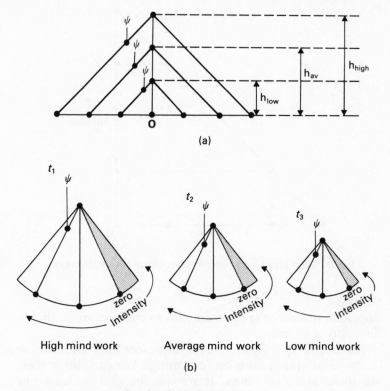

Figure 3.14 Varying levels of mind work
(a) A section through three cones.
h_{high} = high mind work; h_{av} = average mind work;
h_{low} = low mind work
(b) The complete cones

Concentration

The next idea is of great importance to the *map*. It is that of concentration, i.e. concentrating attention or concentrating attention units on things. Consider Figure 3.15, which shows the usual triangle.

At the point Q there are more attention units than things. At the point P there are more things than attention units. If we suppose that there are very few of each at both these points, we can show how the ratio between things and attention units differs at each of them, as shown in Figure 3.16.

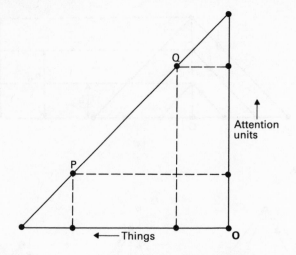

Figure 3.15 Things and attention units in different ratios

Diffusion
This term involves the opposite idea to concentration, that of diffusion of attention.

The diagrams in Figure 3.16(a) represent the concentration of twelve attention units on four things. For each thing there are three attention units. If we assume that at least one attention unit is needed by each thing, then there are two surplus attention units per thing. On the other hand the diagrams in Figure 3.16(b) show the opposite. There are twelve things, but only four attention units to share them, or 'diffuse' among them. So, for each group of three things, there is only one attention unit. Putting it another way, we can say that there is a negative surplus, or deficit, of two attention units for every three things.

The importance of the concentration of attention
My basic idea here is that, in order to think clearly and productively, we need to concentrate our attention. In order to 'grasp' things firmly as we think about them, in order to be sure about the things that we recognize in the outside world or that we retrieve from memory, and in order to be able to store memories that are themselves clear and definite, we need a

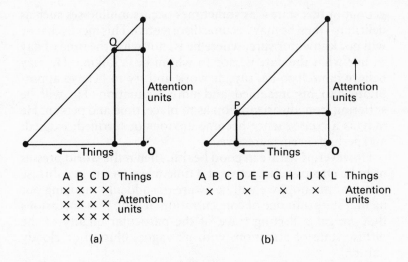

Figure 3.16 Concentration and diffusion of attention units
   (a) Concentration, when things < attention units
   (b) Diffusion, when things > attention units

surplus of attention units – we need to 'concentrate our attention'.

When faced with a difficult task we sometimes concentrate upon it deliberately and put aside other tasks which might distract our attention. 'Please don't talk to me!' we may exclaim, 'I need all the attention I've got.' When we want to make sure of something, to make certain about it, similarly, we concentrate upon it. If we do not do so we may be forced, later, to admit that we are not sure, because we were not paying enough attention at the time.

The consequences of diffusion of attention
Conversely, diffusion of attention means that we cannot grasp things clearly and effectively and with certainty. It means that our perceptions, our thoughts and our memories will be blurred and vague, or even, if we are under pressure, confused. If the world presses someone to be active and effective when he is in a diffuse state of attention, and when he cannot

get out of this state – as sometimes occurs in illnesses such as delirium – then he may become disoriented. This means that he will not know, for sure, where he is, nor what the time of day is, nor what the date is, nor to whom he is talking. He may believe himself to be, say, at work and try to behave appropriately to his imagined and unreal situation. He will be suffering from disorientation as to place, time and person. He may as a consequence become anxious or terrified; excited; and perhaps even aggressive.

However, if we are in good health, then if the world presses us to be effective and active at a time when we are in a diffuse state of attention, we will be aware of suddenly changing our mental state into one of concentration. It is on these occasions that we get a fleeting trace of the particular quality of the diffuse state of attention, with its vague, blurred or cloudy nature.

We are very familiar with such normal, healthy, diffuse states and call them daydreams. They must be distinguished, however, from periods of intense concentrated thinking during which, also, a person may become unaware of his surroundings. This distinction will be discussed again shortly when I raise the question of 'on-line' and 'off-line' thinking.

Diffuse states may be beneficial in several ways, e.g. as part of relaxation and as an aid to initiative and creative thinking.

A peculiar point on the *map* between concentrated and diffused attention
On Figure 3.17 there is a point R at which things and attention units are equal. There can be, therefore, neither a surplus of attention units nor a deficit or scarcity of them at this point. There can be neither concentration of attention nor diffusion of attention at this point. At zero intensity it is called the Zero State or Z-state. (See Figure 3.19.) This is a very important place on the *map*.

The concentration ratio
I can now introduce a second Rule, as follows:

Rule 2: $\dfrac{\text{attention units}}{\text{things}} = \text{concentration ratio}$

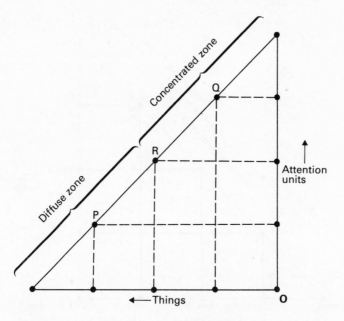

Figure 3.17 A point between concentration and diffusion

From Rule 2 it follows that, at point R, the concentration ratio is 1 because attention units are equal to things. Similarly, points higher up the long side of the triangle, such as Q, have a concentration ratio which is greater than 1. This can be written >1. On the other hand, below R the concentration ratio is less than 1, which can be written <1. At the two limits, where things are either zero or maximal, the concentration ratio is either infinite or zero. These ratios are shown in Figure 3.18. I call states where the concentration ratio is >1 'concentrated' and those where it is <1 'diffuse'.

Two zones, a concentrated zone and a diffuse zone, are shown in Figure 3.18. Now, consider letting the point R, where the concentration ratio is 1, rotate through a complete circle on the triangular 'gate'. It will mark out a circle halfway up the side of the cone, as shown in Figure 3.19.

Two points are marked by a letter ψ (psi) at t_1 and t_2. These are in the concentrated and the diffuse zones respectively.

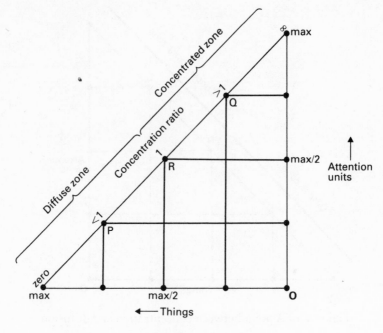

Figure 3.18 The concentration ratio.

$$\frac{\text{attention units}}{\text{things}} = \text{concentration ratio}$$

These points might represent someone who falls into a day-dream. Note that the diffuse zone has been stippled with dots and that, like the concentrated zone, it extends all the way around the cone on both the pleasant and the unpleasant sides.

On-line and off-line cones

In order to be able to represent both on-line and off-line thinking, as discussed earlier, I use two separate cones, as shown in Figure 3.20. The oblong box represents the brain and the rest of the body. The two cones, representing mental states, are placed on top of the box. The place where the two cones touch the box represents the mind–body relation. The nature

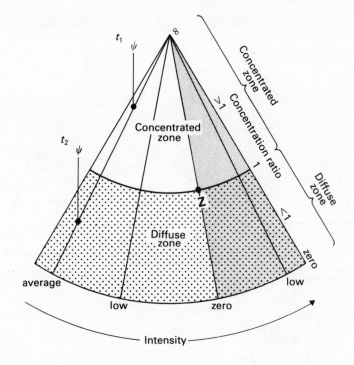

Figure 3.19 The circle halfway up the cone. Point **Z** is at zero
        intensity

of this relation is one of the unsolved problems of philosophy.
(See Campbell, 1970; Eccles, 1977; Fodor, 1981.)

The body interacts with the outside world. Corresponding
to this on-line function of the body is the on-line cone, which I
place at the same end of the box.

At the other end is the off-line cone. I put two arrows on the
top of the box, between the cones, to represent a flow of
information between the on-line and off-line cones by way of a
corresponding flow of nerve-impulses in the brain. I put a
single time – in this case t_1 – to indicate that both the
representative points belong to the same person who experiences, at any particular clock time such as this, both on-line
and off-line mental states.

The off-line cone recalls the idea of the 'mind's eye'.

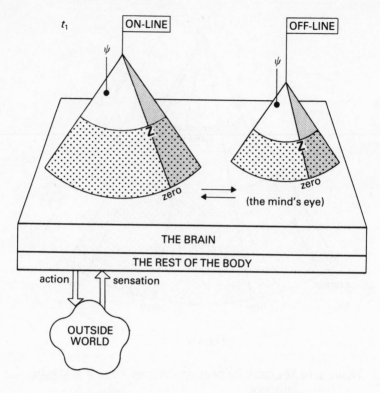

Figure 3.20 On-line and off-line cones

Sleep
To represent sleep I merely add a 'banner' between the cones, as shown in Figure 3.21. This topic will be discussed later in Chapter 4. The time is now t_2.

Spiral lines on the cone
It is now possible to draw some spiral lines on the cone, as shown in Figure 3.22. The representative point ψ is seen from two different points of view, both at the same time, t_1. (The vertex is now labelled V for The Void.) These spirals represent equations which make the level of intensity proportional to the difference between things and attention units. The shape of the spirals is easier to grasp if they are projected vertically down

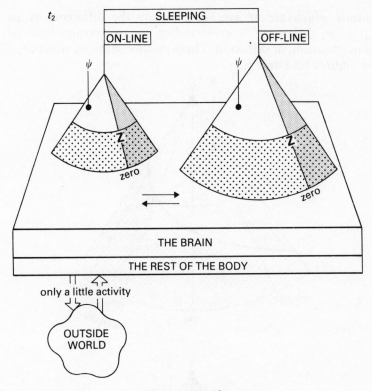

Figure 3.21 Sleep

onto the base of the cone, as in Figure 3.23. (The point **V** now coincides with the Origin, **O**.)

Note that where the spirals are at points of maximal intensity then either things or attention units are maximal; and that attention units or things are correspondingly zero. At these points, at the vertex of the cone and at a point on the rim of its base, the difference between things and attention units is maximal. At one, attention units are maximal while things are zero; at the other, things are maximal while attention units are zero. The latter point is called #**MAX** or diffuse **MAX**. See Figures 8.2 and 12.8. At the point shown on the small circle, halfway up the cone, at **Z**, the intensity is zero. At this point the concentration ratio is 1 because things equal attention units, and so the difference between them is zero. At points on the spirals which are at average intensity the difference is an 'average' difference, corresponding to an average level of concentration, or diffusion. These relationships are illustrated by Figures 3.22 and 3.23.

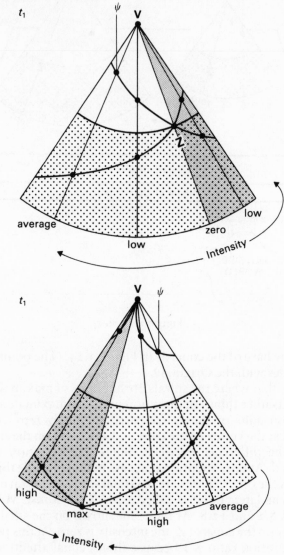

Figure 3.22 Spiral lines on the cone

It would probably help some readers to follow the argument if they drew some triangles and marked surpluses and deficits of attention units on them and related these to the spirals on the cone. Readers may also find it helpful to look at Appendix II now, or, if they have access to a suitable computer, Appendix I, which is a computer graphics program.

3.2 The geometry of the *map*

In the last section I built up the *map* from its component parts, the main variables. These variables were all mental variables.

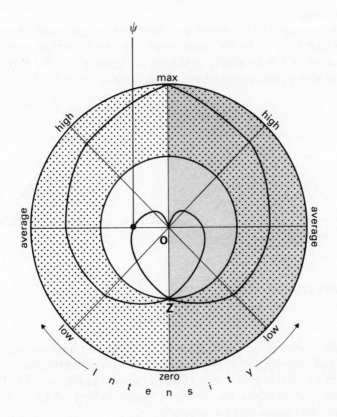

Figure 3.23 The spirals projected down onto the base of the cone. V now coincides with O

I am now going to build up the *map* in a completely different way. I am going to draw the cone as a purely geometrical figure. Then I will 'interpret' its variables in mental terms. Thus, I will say 'for parameter *k* read mind work', and so on.

The point of repeating this building process is to allow the reader to see the structure of the *map* differently, to consider the geometry in the abstract, as a 'calculus', and to see the calculus being 'interpreted' in a particular way, as a map which is a 'model' of mental states. This approach to the structure of a scientific theory — seeing models as interpretations of a calculus — is derived from Braithwaite (1953).

The cone

The cone used in the *map* has a base with radius *r* and a height *h* which is equal to *r*. Consequently, the angle at the vertex of the cone is a right angle, as shown in Figure 3.24. The Origin, O, is at the centre of the base of the cone.

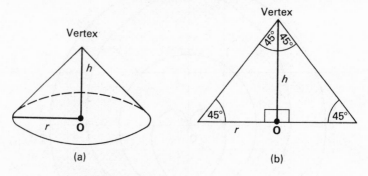

Figure 3.24 A right-angled cone
           (a) The cone, seen obliquely from above
           (b) A vertical section through the cone

Any point P, on the surface of the cone, can be described by θ_p and either r_p or h_p. θ_p is an angular co-ordinate measured from a radial line defined as θ_{zero}, as shown in Figure 3.25. The cone is defined as the locus of points where $h + r = k$ (a particular value of a parameter).

If we consider the point P_1, where $r_{p_1} = h_{p_1}$, and we imagine that this point rotates around the surface of the cone for all

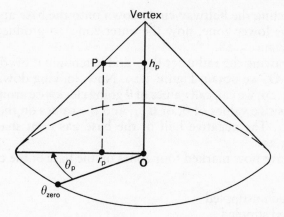

Figure 3.25 The three co-ordinates of a point, P, on the surface of a
cone

values of θ, then we will have drawn a circle around the cone
halfway up its side, and with a radius of half the radius of the
base of the cone, as shown in Figure 3.26.

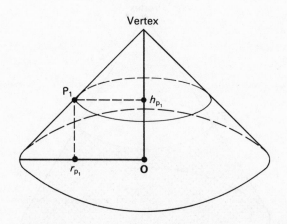

Figure 3.26 Rotating a point P_1, where $r_{p_1} = h_{p_1}$

We can mark the zone below this halfway circle on the
surface of the cone by stippling it with dots, as shown in Figure
3.27.

Projecting the halfway circle down onto the base and stippling the lower zone, now the outer zone, so produced, we obtain Figure 3.28.

By drawing the radius at θ_{zero} and extending it beyond the Origin, O, we obtain Figure 3.29. Now, looking down onto Figure 3.29, we can call values of θ going clockwise around the base positive values of θ, or θ_{pos}, and the values on the other side θ_{neg}. The negative half of the base has been shaded in Figure 3.29.

We have now marked four zones on the base of the cone as follows:

unshaded unstippled
unshaded stippled
shaded unstippled
shaded stippled

These can also be seen on the surface of the cone itself as shown in Figure 3.30. The size of the cone can be varied by varying a parameter, the radius of the base, without altering the relative

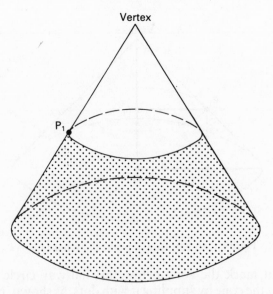

Figure 3.27 The lower zone stippled with dots

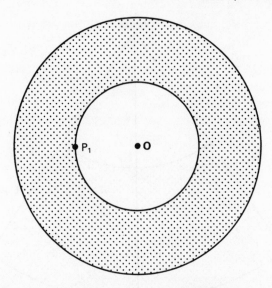

Figure 3.28 The lower zone projected down onto the base as an
outer zone

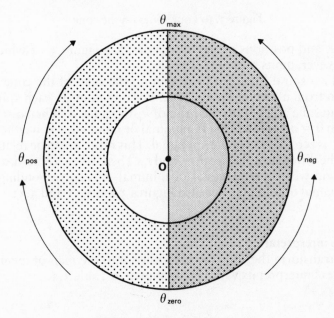

Figure 3.29 θ_{zero} and θ_{max}

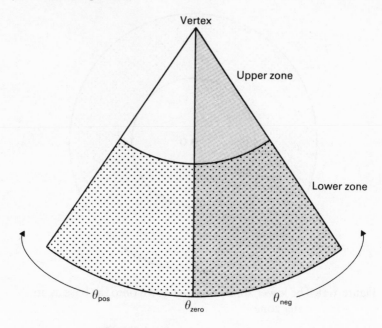

Figure 3.30 Four zones on the cone

sizes and positions of the four zones. See Figure 3.14 which, however, omits the stippled zones.

Two spiral lines can be drawn on the sides of the cone as seen from above in Figure 3.32. For any point P, each spiral relates the angle θ_p to the ratio of h_p to r_p, i.e. a. When $a = 1$, then $\theta = 0°$, and when a is maximal or minimal, when either r or h is zero, $\theta = 180°$, i.e. maximal. This ratio, a, can be related to the difference d between h_p and r_p. Then, when d is zero, $a = 1$, and when d is maximal or minimal, a is correspondingly maximal or minimal. See also Figures 3.25, 3.31 and 3.32.

The interpretation of the cone

To transform the cone just described into the *map* of mental states I interpret its variables as shown in Table 3.3.

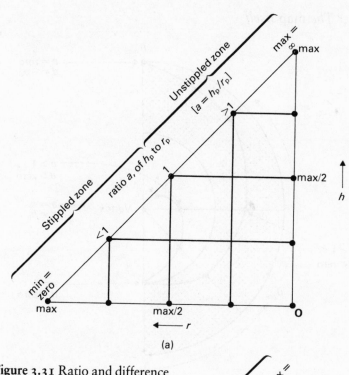

Figure 3.31 Ratio and difference

(a) Ratio $a = \dfrac{h_p}{r_p}$

(b) Difference $d = h_p - r_p$

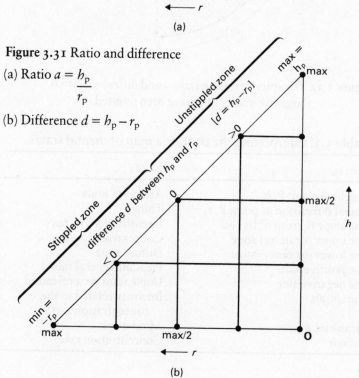

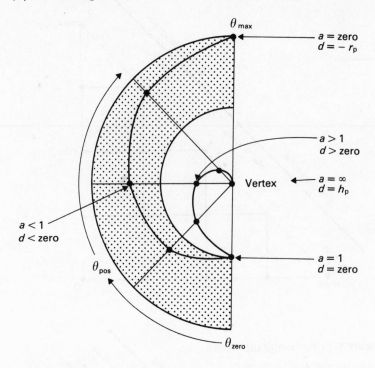

Figure 3.32 The spirals relating ratio *a* and difference *d* to θ.
Negative values of θ have been omitted

Table 3.3. Interpreting the cone as a *map* of mental states

For . . .	Read . . .
Height at point P, h_p	Attention units
Radial dimension at point P, r_p	Things
The angle θ, from 0° to 180°	Intensity, zero to max
The upper (or inner) zone	Concentrated zone
The lower (or outer) zone	Diffuse zone
The positive side	Pleasant general mood
The negative side	Unpleasant general mood
The spirals	Intensity related to the concentration ratio
Parameter *k*	Mind work
Ratio *a*	Concentration ratio

The previous section, Section 3.1, built up the same cone but not in an abstract geometrical manner. At the end of Section 3.1 the cone was the same as the one produced above by interpreting the abstract geometry of the cone, as shown in Figure 3.33.

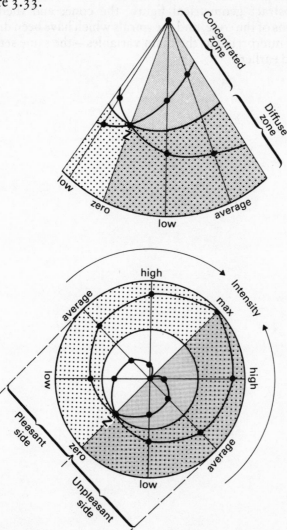

Figure 3.33 The interpretation of the cone as a *map* of mental states

3.3 Chapter summary

The *map* is built up, step by step, from the main variables discussed in Chapters 1 and 2. Extra variables are added.

Then the process is repeated, but this time the *map* is built up as an abstract geometrical figure, the cone, and then the dimensions of the cone, and the spirals which have been drawn on it, are interpreted as the main variables – the same set that were used earlier.

PART THREE

Using the *map* to plot mental states

This part of the book explores ways in which the *map* can be used to plot journeys in the four main types of mental life: ordinary life; mystical states; mental illnesses; and drug states. These are discussed in Chapters 4, 5, 6 and 7 respectively.

Both on-line and off-line functions will be shown in Chapter 4, in Figures 4.3 and 4.4. After that, however, for reasons of simplicity, the distinction between on-line and off-line functions will not be shown until Figures 11.9 and 11.10. (See also Figure 5.2.)

PART THREE

Using the map to plot mental states

Chapter 4

Plotting ordinary life

4.1 The four types of mental life

So far I have discussed two important types of mental life: ordinary life, in Chapter 1, and mystical states, in Chapter 2. If two more types of mental life are added one has a comprehensive system of classification which can encompass any state of mind. These further two types are mental illnesses and drug states. Table 4.1 lists the four types.

Table 4.1 The four types of mental life

Ordinary life
Mystical states
Mental illnesses
Drug states

Ordinary life is interpreted very widely, in the belief that it contains a very wide variety of mental states, some of which are very strange. The question as to whether a person's life is no longer ordinary will involve how often the more unusual states occur and in what sequences; also their duration and intensity.

There are border-zones between ordinary life and the other three types of mental life. What is more, the other three types of mental life have border-zones between themselves, which have been explored by the following:

Zone 4: Aldous Huxley (1954);
Zone 5: John Custance (1951) quoted by Happold (1963);
Zone 6: A. Hofmann (1955) cited by Slater and Roth (1977).
    Also see the quotation in Julien (1978).

These six border-zones are shown in Figure 4.1.

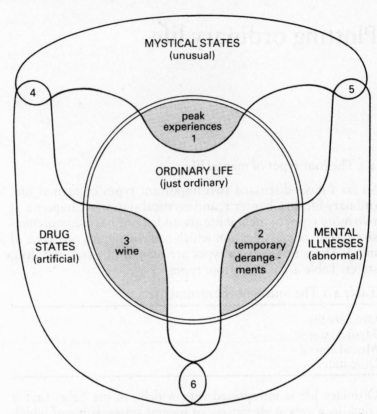

Figure 4.1 The six border-zones between the four types of mental
           life: a Venn diagram

4.2 Some familiar journeys

I am now going to describe some of the familiar journeys on
which a person goes, every day and night, and also a few of the
less familiar journeys which are, nonetheless, part of ordinary
life.

Alert, relaxed and daydreaming states

It has been suggested that during our waking states of mind we
continue to show a pattern which corresponds to the periods
of paradoxical, or rapid eye movement (REM), sleep that

occur about every ninety minutes during the night (see Oswald, 1970). During the day, it is suggested, we take a 'break' about every ninety minutes and, typically, have a snack. These periods are said to be ones of relaxation, interposed between more concentrated times.

Following this idea, I assume that we tend to alternate between periods of concentrated thinking and either relaxed thinking which is still within the concentrated zone or thinking which is of the diffuse kind, that is to say, daydreaming. A brief sequence of mental states which illustrates this idea is shown in Figure 4.2

For convenience the *map* can be used in the form of its projection down onto the base of the cone. The point labelled ψ (psi) represents the person experiencing the states portrayed at a series of clock times, t_1, t_2, t_3 and so on. Notice that the mind work level has been varied. From now on the *map* will be presented in this simpler form.

Both forms, a cone and the base of the cone, can be used in computer graphical representations of the *map*. In Appendix I the disc is obtained by 'looking down' on the cone from directly above, as shown in Figure I.8. The basic pattern, shown in Figure 4.2 can then be modified and elaborated in many ways.

For example, various extra variables can be added at different times: headache, hunger (before breakfast, say), restlessness, anxiety (specific or general), irritability, amusement, self-consciousness, and so on.

Then again, mind work and the concentration ratio can be modified. Some people feel very alert on waking. Others feel lethargic and in an unpleasant mood for some time, until their 'black cloud' lifts, helped perhaps by coffee. Such people may feel most awake in the late evening.

On-line and off-line functions
In order to be able to represent some of the richness and complexity of even the most ordinary day we need to be able to show on-line and off-line functions. A cone or base of the cone is needed for each function. The right-hand cone can be labelled *off-line*. (See Figure 4.3(a).)

Consider a man who gets up and starts to shave, performing

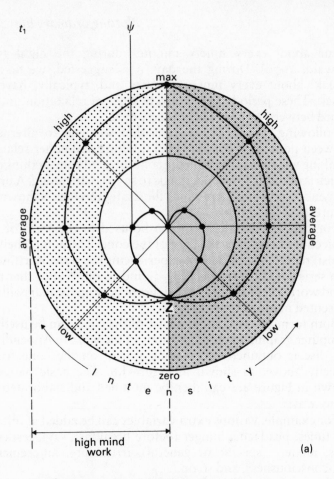

Figure 4.2 Alert, relaxed and daydreaming states

(a) Alert, with high mind work: intensity – average; concentration – average; general mood – pleasant. No extra variables

(b) Alert, with average mind work: intensity – average; concentration – average; general mood – pleasant. No extra variables. This is the Golden A-state

(c) Relaxed, with low mind work: intensity – average; concentration – low; general mood – pleasant. No extra variables

(d) Daydreaming, with average mind work: diffusion (of attention) – average; general mood – pleasant. No extra variables

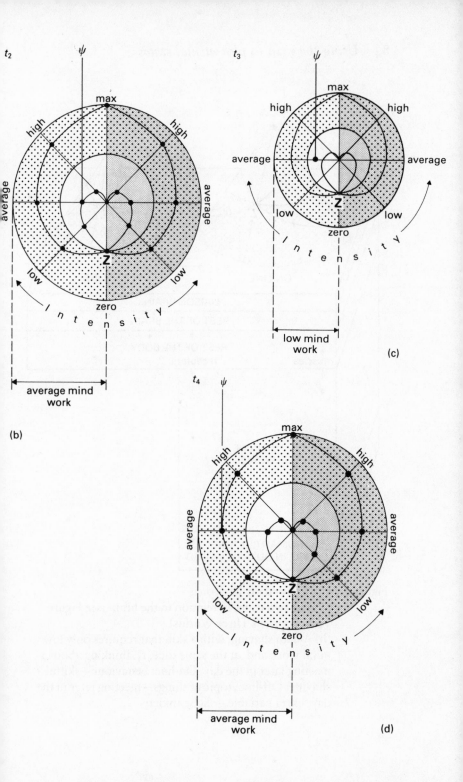

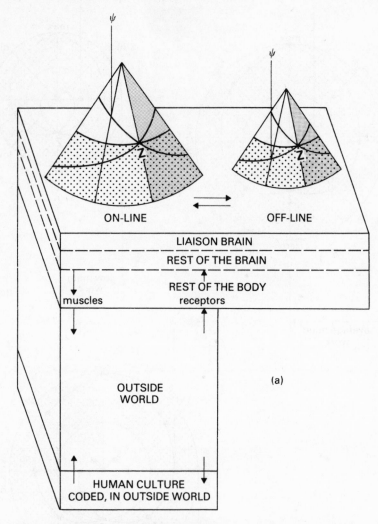

Figure 4.3 On-line and off-line cones
(a) The two cones in relation to the brain (see Figure
10.4, Popper's Three Worlds)
(b) A man shaving, with a skill that requires only low
mind work and, at the same time, t_1, thinking about a
meeting later in the day. On-line: behaviour – skilful
shaving. Off-line: topic of things – meeting later in the
day; extra variable – slight anxiety

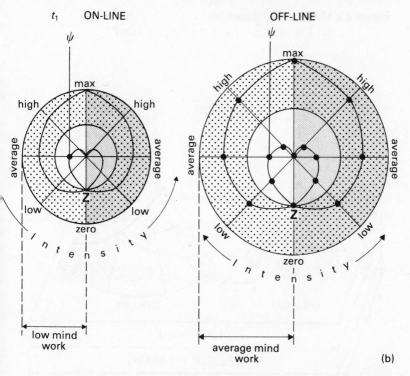

that familiar skill with very little mind work, as shown on the *on-line* cone. At the same time, t_1, he is thinking about a meeting that he is due to attend later in the day, and imagines himself addressing it. This is concentrated, *off-line* thinking, with average mind work. And so on. (See Figure 4.3 (b).)

Sleeping and dreaming

Figure 4.4 represents a sequence of states which might be experienced by a person during sleep, showing 'orthodox' and paradoxical (REM) sleep. It includes pleasant dreams and an unpleasant dream, that is to say a 'nightmare'.

The basic sleeping pattern can be varied by changing the times at which the person goes to sleep and wakes up. Also he can be shown waking up in the middle of the night.

We have now established a considerable repertory of possible sequences of mental states in ordinary waking and sleeping. Characteristic sequences can be noted, recorded and

Figure 4.4 Sleeping and dreaming
(a) The two cones and the sleeping label

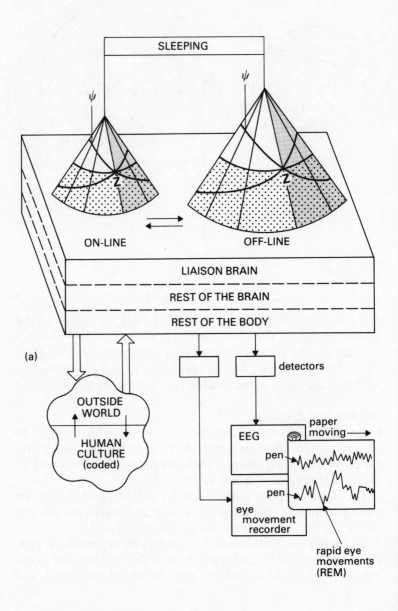

(b) Non-rapid eye movement (non-REM) sleep.
Behaviour: sleeping posture; eyes closed; some bodily
movements; some words may be uttered.
Electroencephalograph (EEG); stages I to IV, large slow
waves. On-line: low mind work; concentration — low;
monitoring outside world. Off-line: general mood –
pleasant; mind work – average; concentration – average;
dreaming (not vividly); topic of things – (on recall)
vague, a conversation with somebody about the news
(say)

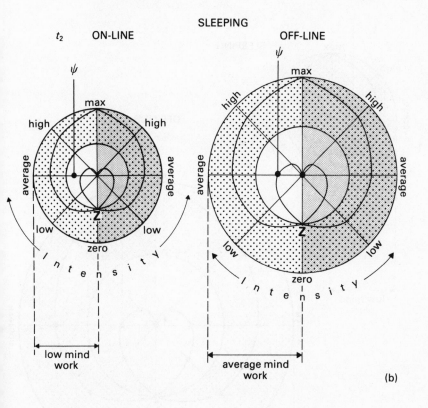

(b)

(c) Vivid nightmare; rapid eye movement (REM) sleep. Behaviour: no bodily movements apart from REM; penile erections. EEG: 'paradoxical', i.e. small irregular waves, as during the waking state. On-line: mind work – low; concentration – low; monitoring the outside world. Off-line: mind work – high; topic of things – (for example) being chased through deep snow at night by wolves, the deep snow preventing escape; extra variables – anxiety and fear; (should both general moods be unpleasant?).

(d) Pleasant eerie dream: REM; On-line: monitoring the outside world as for (c). Off-line mind work – average; off-line intensity – low; concentration is appropriate to the intensity. Behaviour: as for (c). EEG: as for (c). Off-line: topic of things – (for example) walking through a beautiful building with panelled rooms painted white and gold, to the sound of rain in the trees outside the windows, the rooms forming some sort of maze. Yet the dream, though uncanny, is not unpleasant

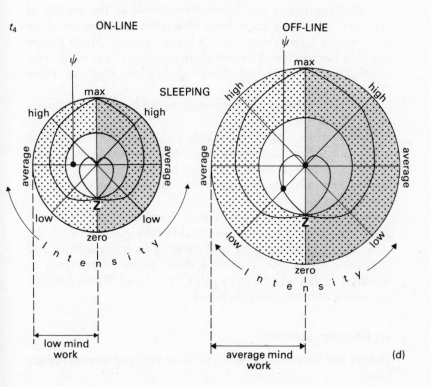

stored. For example, a particular person who sleeps very little and feels very alert on waking displays a particular sequence which can be noted and recorded.

Border-zones

As shown above, in Figure 4.1, ordinary life has border-zones with mental illness, with mysticism and with drug states. Brief episodes within these border-zones could be shown. For example, a Peak Experience could occur during the waking state, with a rise in intensity.

Peak Experiences can happen to people in the middle of ordinary life. They have been described and discussed by Marghanita Laski (1961) in her book *Ecstasy*. Much poetry has also been devoted to this theme, notably that of Wordsworth. See *The Oxford Book of English Mystical Verse* (Nicholson and Lee, 1917).

The most familiar border-zone is probably with drugs, especially alcohol.

Mental illness has a less easily defined border-zone with ordinary life, but in his play *The Family Reunion*, T. S. Eliot (1939) portrays a man who can be seen as living in this border-zone and, during the course of the drama, being released from it.

Ordinary life has what Gavin Lambert (1975) calls a *dangerous edge*. This is an internal border-zone between the safer parts of ordinary life and some of its more sinister and insecure regions. He illustrates these zones by referring to novelists such as Ambler (1940), Conrad and Wilkie Collins, and to the film director Hitchcock.

4.3 Chapter summary

The six border-zones between the four types of mental life are listed.

Then some familiar journeys are described within ordinary life, between alert, relaxed and daydreaming states. On-line and off-line functions are shown and, with their aid, sleeping and dreaming are plotted.

The border-zones are discussed again, with examples of mental states encountered within them.

Chapter 5

Plotting the mystical path

The mystical path has already been described in Chapter 2 and so the purpose of the present chapter is to portray it on the *map*. When we move on to Chapters 6 and 7 similarities will become apparent between the mystical path and the path of some mental illnesses, notably manic-depressive illness, and some drug-induced states, notably the psychedelic drug-induced states known as 'good and bad trips'. However, important as these similarities are, there are also dissimilarities.

5.1 The best-known mystical path

Following the description given in Chapter 2, the best-known mystical path can be portrayed, starting at an ordinary, alert, but attached mental state, as in Figure 5.1. For the sake of simplicity and because of the lack of information about sleeping states along the mystical path I will only consider waking states.

I have not shown any of the many possible pitfalls along the mystical path. However, the mystics can become excited and conceited. They can experience hallucinations, both visual and auditory. They can move across to the dark side of the *map*. Another hazard is for them to become lethargic, and lose concentration when meditating.

5.2 The best-known mystical path as a ring of landmarks

The mystics have produced a vast literature describing their journeys around the mystical path: how they set out; and what

Figure 5.1 The best-known mystical path
(a) Starting at the Average State, with attachment $|\mathbf{A}|$. Main variables: awake; mind work – average; mood – pleasant; intensity – average; concentration – average; time – t_1. Special variable: attachment. See Krishnamurti in Lutyens (1970); and Saint-Exupéry (1945)
(b) The Outsider State at $|\mathbf{A}|$. Main variables: awake; mind work – average; mood – pleasant; intensity – average; concentration – average; time – t_2. Extra variable: anxiety. Special variable: attachment breached. See Camus (1942) and Wilson (1956)

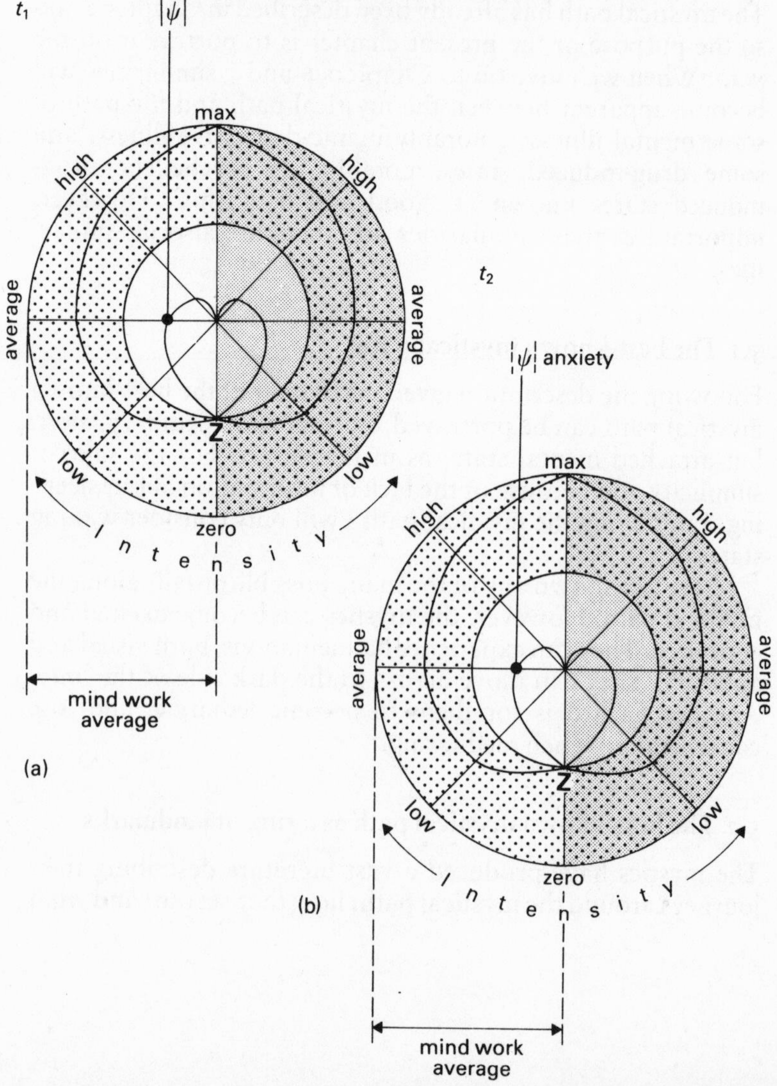

(c) Meditation at |**A**|. Main variables: awake; mind work – average; mood – pleasant; intensity – average; concentration – raised; time – t_3. Special variable: attachment breached. See Patanjali in Stephen (1957).

(d) A Peak Experience at **P**. Main variables: awake; mind work – average; mood – pleasant; intensity – raised; concentration – raised; time – t_4. See Traherne in Happold (1963)

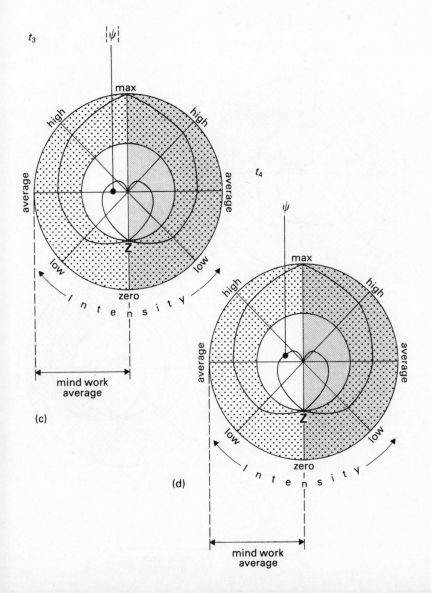

(e) A Mystical State Proper at **M**. Main variables:
awake; mind work – average; mood – pleasant; intensity
– high; concentration – high; time – t_5. See Bucke in
James (1902) or Happold (1963)

(f) Point of No Return, between the Mystical State
Proper and The Void. Main variables: awake; mind
work – average; mood – pleasant; intensity – very high;
concentration – very high; time – t_6. See Koestler (1954)

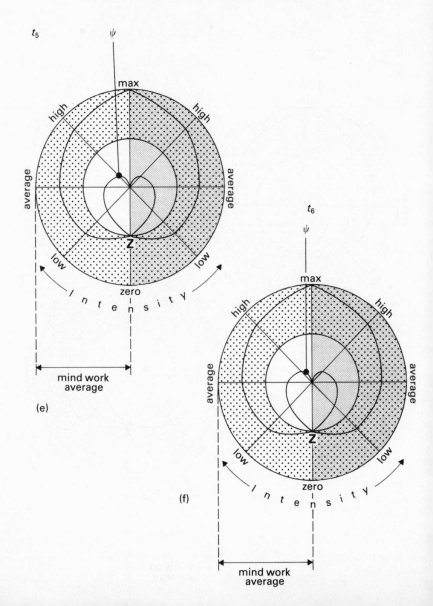

(g) The Void at **V**. Main variables: awake; mind work – average; mood – not applicable; intensity – maximal; concentration – maximal; time – t_7. Extra variables: not applicable. See Koestler (1954) and al-Ghazali in Happold (1963). This State changes at once. See (h)

(h) The Origin at **O**. Main variables: mind work – zero; all others – not applicable; time – t_8. Extra variables: not applicable. (See Figures 3.22 and 3.23 for the relation between **V** and **O**.)

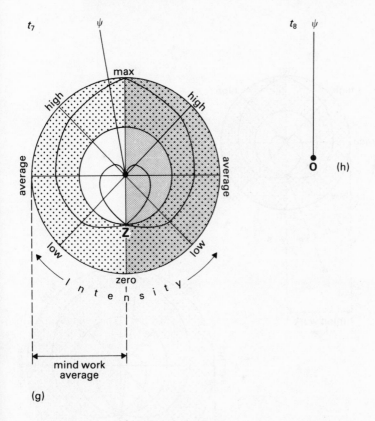

(g)

(i) Zero State at **Z**. Main variables: awake; mind work –
low; mood – not applicable; intensity – zero;
concentration – zero; concentration ratio – 1; time – t_9.
Extra variables: not applicable

(j) Zero State with mind work average at **Z**. Main
variables: awake; mind work – average; mood – not
applicable; intensity – zero; concentration – zero;
concentration ratio – 1; time – t_{10}. Extra variables: not
applicable

(k) The end of the path (?) at **A***. The Average State with enlightenment. Main variables: awake; mind work – average; mood – pleasant; intensity – average; concentration – average; time – t_{11}. Special variable: enlightenment. See Chuang Tzu in Watts (1957)

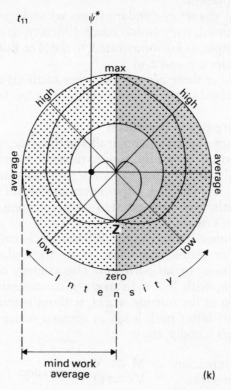

(k)

happened to them, on the way and at their destination. These descriptions, taken one at a time, are made up of 'soft data'. However, when taken together, a remarkably consistent picture emerges.

It shows a route through a wide variety of mental states. These can remain fairly clear and undistorted even when most intense. The mystics can, however, wander off the route.

This route, the mystical path, can be seen as a ring of landmarks, to which the irregular and distorted paths of mental illness and drugs can be referred.

5.3 Other routes

What I have called the best-known mystical path is typical both of the Raja Yoga of Patanjali and of the Western Christian mystical tradition: concentration leads to meditation and contemplation.

I think the set of standard stages which I have drawn up can also be fitted, without too much difficulty, to other traditions; for example, as I demonstrated, to the 'Ten Bulls' (Reps, 1957) (see Tables 2.8 and 2.9).

However there are various other methods which do not fit my standard stages so neatly. Here are a few of them.

The two paths of Buddhism

Buddhism contains two parallel paths. One, the path of concentration or *samadhi*, passes through a series of *jhanas* or 'trances' which include experiences of bliss and rapture. These can be related to Peak Experiences and Mystical States Proper. This path uses 'one-pointed' concentration and resembles Patanjali's method.

The other path is quite different. It is called the path of insight or *prajna* and uses, as its method, what is called mindfulness, or *satipatthana*. This consists of gently paying attention, with less than average concentration, to what is going on in the outside world, without reacting to it. Eventually this latter path leads to *nirvana* which I identify with my stages 6 and 7, thus:

6 Contemplation $M \rightleftarrows V$
7 Return to the $V \Longrightarrow O$ *nirvana*
  Origin

The main point about reaching *nirvana* is that this is said to change the personality. The difference between the above two methods is shown in Figure 5.2.

So far as I understand it, the route to *nirvana* is via the concentration method followed by the mindfulness method. I would not have expected that: I would have expected the order to be reversed. However, it occurs to me that perhaps the two methods can be practised simultaneously, with mindfulness on-line and concentration off-line? The two representative points could then be shown reaching the two doorways to the Origin, O, simultaneously, V, off-line and Z on-line.

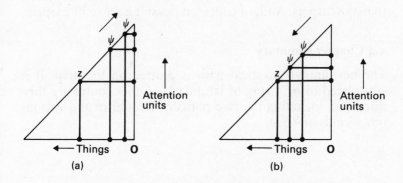

(a)   (b)

Figure 5.2 The two methods used in Buddhist meditation: concentration and mindfulness. (a) Concentration (*samādhi*). (b) Mindfulness (*satipatthana*).

The *satori* of Zen Buddhism

Zen *satori* is sudden. Accounts of it sound like the sudden onset of a Peak Experience. I am not sure whether it has an effect on personality, like reaching *nirvana*. See Reps (1957), Herrigel (1953), Blythe (1942). If it does, then perhaps it is an instantaneous passage around the mystical path to A*. Perhaps, even, it is a path that goes from A, via Z, to O, then back again to A*?

Various other kinds of Yoga

Apart from the classic Raja Yoga of Patanjali, there are various other methods. For example there is the Yoga of devotion, Bhakti Yoga: see, for example, the devotion of Lucius to the goddess Isis, as recounted by Apuleius (1950); and the later cult of the Virgin Mary, also Queen of Heaven.

Another kind of Yoga is the Yoga of discrimination. This is a philosophical sort of Yoga. It is described in Chapter IV of the *Bhagavad-Gita* (Prabhavananda and Isherwood, 1947).

Another kind of Yoga is like the informal method of instruction which is known, in industry, as 'sitting with Nelly'. You go and learn how to make carpets. You have to choose your teacher with care and he won't teach you anything except how to make carpets. And, of course, it doesn't have to be carpets.

5.4 Chapter summary

The best-known mystical path is plotted on the *map*. It is considered to be a ring of landmarks. Other routes are then discussed, including the two paths of Buddhism and various other kinds of Yoga.

Chapter 6

Plotting mental illnesses

Different mental illnesses show characteristic sequences, of onset and progress, of their particular set of symptoms and signs. A symptom is what the patient complains of, such as 'feeling anxious' or being in 'low spirits' or having a compulsion to keep checking, say, that the door is locked. A sign is what is observed by the doctors and nurses, such as a sad facial expression or tone of voice, agitated behaviour, compulsive behaviour, and so on.

In this chapter I sketch very briefly some of the main mental illnesses by plotting some typical mental states encountered during them. Further details may be found in large psychiatric textbooks such as that of Slater and Roth (1977), or smaller ones such as that of Stafford-Clark and Smith (1980), and in related books such as those by Martin (1981) and Jaspers (1913). Descriptions of their own illnesses, by patients, will be found in Kaplan's (1964) anthology, and in Sutherland (1976) and Waugh (1957). The latter gives a fictional account of a personal experience of a paranoid type of illness, possibly due to poisoning by a self-administered medicine containing bromide and chloral.

6.1 A warning

Readers who have worries about their own or other people's mental states are strongly advised to consult their doctor. Self-diagnosis is a very hazardous procedure and the information given in this book is not detailed enough for diagnosis.

Nevertheless this book may help some people to understand mental illnesses better. In particular, the *map* may remove some of the fear of the unknown by relating some states of mind in mental illness to the more familiar states of mind in ordinary life. However, some of the mental states encountered in mental illness are very unfamiliar and, for that reason, especially frightening. Merely to realize that such states are well-known to doctors and nurses, and have been experienced many times before by other patients, may itself relieve some of a person's anxiety about them.

This chapter might even be useful to a doctor or nurse who is trying to explain to a patient the nature of his illness and how treatment may improve the prospect.

6.2 Some typical mental illnesses

To illustrate each of the illnesses that I have chosen, I will portray, on the *map*, one or more mental states to show some of the characteristic features of the particular illness. Figure 6.1(a) shows a normal alert waking mental state to represent the patient in a state of good health, before the illness. (On-line and off-line cones will not be distinguished from each other in this Chapter, or Chapter 7.)

Depressive illness

Figure 6.1 shows a healthy person gradually becoming ill, with a loss of mind work and then a loss of concentration and a shift over to the unpleasant side of the *map*. Various extra variables are added including anxiety, delusions and hallucinations. Concentration becomes *relatively* low in view of high intensity. The representative point is then outside the inner spiral. With the aid of more Figures the patient could be shown getting better after being given anti-depressant drugs. Chesterton (1929) gives a vivid description of a mild depressive illness in one of his short stories.

For severe depressive illness see Sutherland (1976) and Custance (1951). Also see Mitchell (1981).

Mania

Figure 6.2 shows the course of a manic illness with increasing mind work, a loss of concentration and the addition of a

Figure 6.1 Depressive illness
(a) Before the onset of the illness: the Golden A-state
(b) The illness begins: mood – unpleasant; concentration
– low (relatively); intensity – average; mind work –
average. Extra variables: anxiety (often present); sleep
disturbance – difficulty in going to sleep, bad dreams,
early waking; loss of weight; loss of appetite

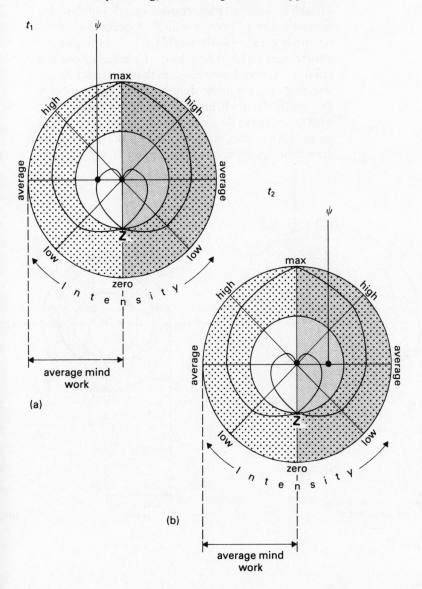

(c) The intensity increases on the dark side:
concentration – relatively low; mind work – average.
Extra variables: as for (b); plus, often, agitation,
delusions of guilt and unworthiness, suicidal ideas,
hypochondriacal ideas

(d) Mind work is reduced to low: intensity – high on the
dark side; concentration – relatively low. Extra
variables: as for (c); plus retarded speech and thought;
rumination upon a very few ideas. Aspects of mind
(intensely dark): $-K$, the world has no meaning or
significance, his life is pointless; $-U$, he feels alone and a
failure; $-E$, time feels useless, in that he cannot do
anything in it, but it also drags; $-L$, the world appears
grey and lifeless; $-B$, his body feels heavy and weary,
with no energy to do anything; $-J$, misery is the
prevailing emotion, and a remorse for the past; $-F$, there
are no choices open, everything is hopeless

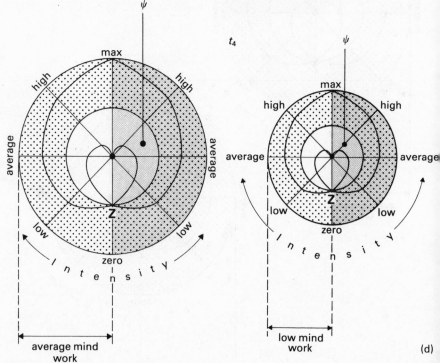

Figure 6.2 Mania

(a) Hypomania: mind work – average; intensity – average to high on the pleasant side; concentration – relatively low. Extra variables: hilarity; talkativeness; enthusiasm for many new plans; occasional irritability; denies having any illness

(b) Full manic state: mind work – high; intensity – high; concentration – relatively low. Extra variables: grandiose ideas; loss of critical sense, leading to imprudent behaviour; insight (that he is ill) is completely lost: overactive; talkative, with 'flight of ideas' from one topic to another, jokes, puns

(c) Dark mental state but with the other symptoms and signs of mania; the mood may keep changing from pleasant to unpleasant, i.e. to (b) and back. Extra variables: tearfulness; otherwise as for (b)

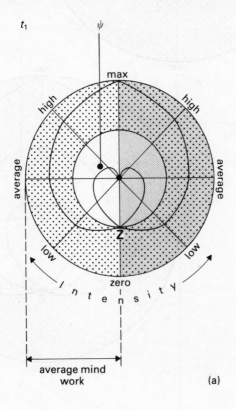

(a)

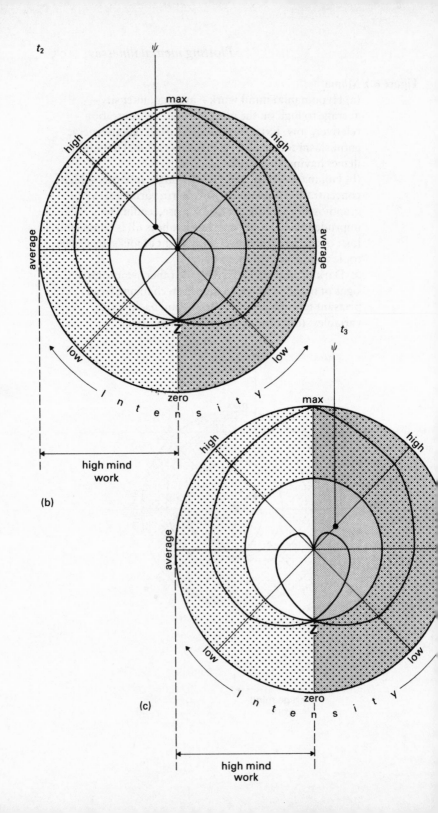

t_2

ψ

max

high   high

average   average

low   low

zero

I n t e n s i t y

high mind
work

(b)

t_3

ψ

max

high   high

average   average

low   low

zero

I n t e n s i t y

high mind
work

(c)

different kind of delusion. The patient could be then shown getting better after being given treatment, say that of the drug lithium carbonate. For a description of an attack of the milder form of mania, called hypomania, see Sutherland (1976).

For severe mania see Custance (1951). With the aid of more Figures the tendency of manic patients to go without sleep, in a constant round of activity, leading to exhaustion, could be shown.

A mixed neurotic illness
Many patients suffer from neurotic illnesses which show a fluctuating course, with many different symptoms and signs. Figure 6.3 illustrates their sort of illness. Treatment is with sedatives if necessary. Also, see Section 6.4, below.

Delirium
Physical disorder of the brain, caused by injury, alcohol or infection, can result in a delirium. Also, the very young and the very old are more prone to develop delirium. The patient shown in Figure 6.4 is suffering from delirium tremens, the trembling delirium that can occur in chronic alcoholism. It occurs, in a person who is physically dependent upon alcohol, when alcohol is withdrawn. It is often preceded by an epileptic fit. Treatment is with fluids, vitamins and sedatives.

Schizophrenia
There are several different kinds of schizophrenia. Figure 6.5 (a) shows a type of schizophrenia in which the patient, although remaining in the 'clear' zone, has bizarre delusions and hallucinations, of a persecutory nature. I also show a different patient, in a catatonic state which I tentatively place at the Zero State. With more Figures, these symptoms could be shown being alleviated by treatment with a phenothiazine drug, such as chlorpromazine.

6.3 Depersonalization and derealization
These two symptoms can occur, transiently, in ordinary life or in its border-zone with mental illness, i.e. area '2' in Figure 4.1. They are illustrated by the fictional, but probably accurate

Figure 6.3 Mixed neurotic illness
(a) Intensity – average; (general) mood – pleasant; mind
work – average; concentration – low. Extra variables:
the following may come and go – anxiety (general),
phobias, tension (feeling 'strung up'), heaviness in the
limbs, disturbances of sleep
(b) Malaise and lethargy: mood – unpleasant; mind
work – low; concentration – low; intensity – average.
Extra variables: lethargy, physical and mental; general
feeling of malaise, being 'out of sorts'

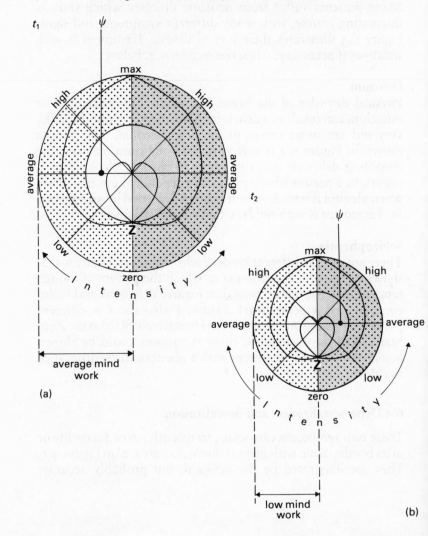

(c) Episode of depersonalization and derealization. Extra variables: depersonalization; derealization; otherwise as for (a). Note drop in intensity

(d) Transient euphoric episode: intensity – between average and high; concentration – relatively low; mind work – average. Transient loss of above extra variables

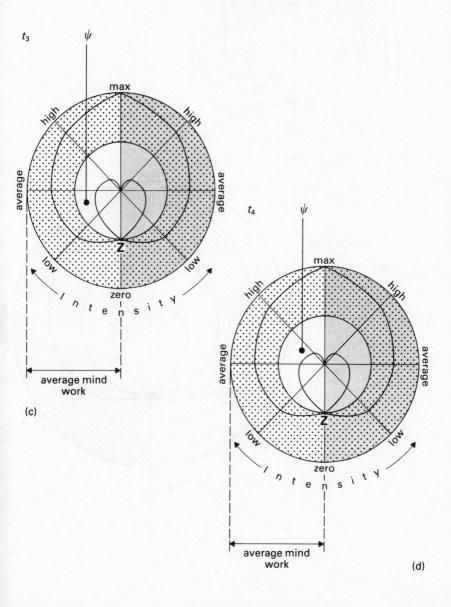

(c)

(d)

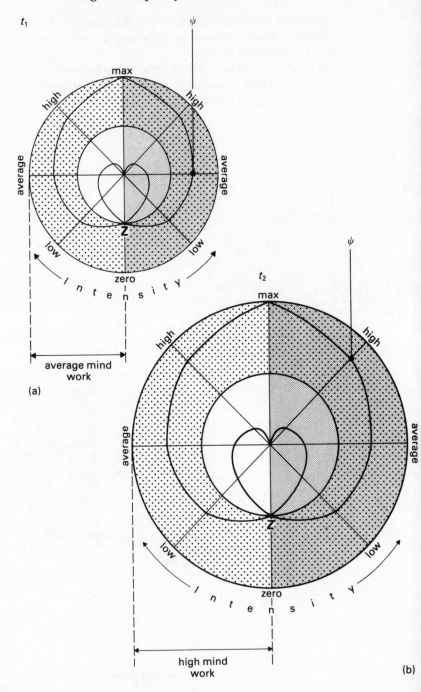

t_1

max

high

high

average

average

low

low

Z

zero

I n t e n s i t y

ψ

average mind
work

(a)

t_2

max

high

high

average

average

low

low

Z

zero

I n t e n s i t y

ψ

high mind
work

(b)

Figure 6.4 Delirium tremens
(a) Period preceding the delirium and possibly following alcoholic withdrawal: attention – diffuse, mood – unpleasant. Extra variables: disorientation; misinterpretation of the environment; apprehension
(b) The delirium itself: mind work – high; mood – unpleasant (may be mixed); attention – very diffuse. Extra variables: fear; excitement with, sometimes, aggression; misinterpreting the environment as hostile; hallucinations (visual and auditory); restlessness

Figure 6.5 Schizophrenia: two different types
(a) Paranoid type: clear mind apart from hallucinations and delusions. Mind work – average; intensity – average; concentration – average. Extra variables: hallucinations, especially auditory, often of one or more voices; delusions, especially of being persecuted; items in newspapers, remarks overheard, and so on, may be held to refer to the patient

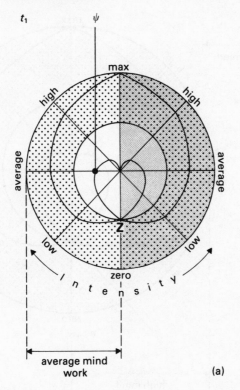

(a)

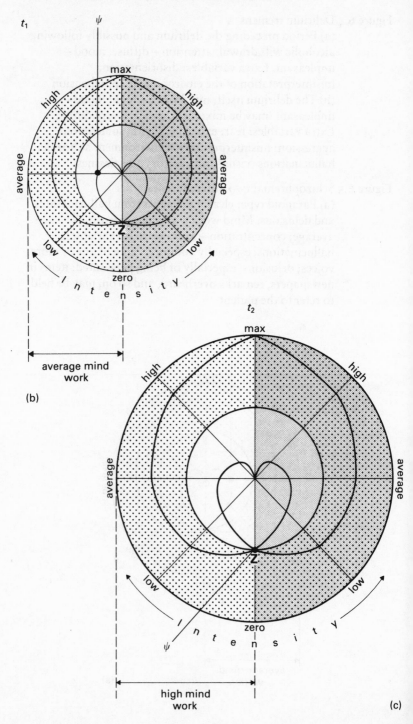

(b) Catatonic type: mind work – average; with catatonic symptoms. Extra variables: strange postures; altered muscular tone ('waxy flexibility'); automatic obedience to every instruction; echolalia, i.e. repeating the last few syllables of everything that is said

(c) Catatonic type: catatonic excitement. This has been located speculatively at the Zero State, **Z**. Mood – indeterminate; intensity – zero. Extra variables: wild excitement; speech disorder, breakdown of meaning to a 'word salad'

(d) Catatonic type: catatonic semi-stupor. This has also been located speculatively at the Zero State, **Z**. Mood – indeterminate; intensity – zero. Extra variables: as for (b); but with mutism; and movements slow.

With further reduction in mind work there is stupor, perhaps with no mental content, although the patient is awake

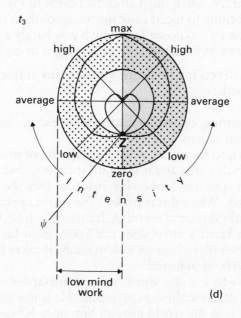

description given by Sartre (1938) which is quoted below. However they also occur in some kinds of schizophrenia. Depersonalization is when a person feels unreal. Derealization is when the world appears unreal.

Consider the experience described by the narrator in Sartre's (1938) novel *Nausea*.

> Something has happened to me: I can't doubt that any more. It came as an illness does, not like an ordinary certainty, not like anything obvious. I felt a little strange, a little awkward, and that was all.
>
> There is something new, for example, about my hands, a certain way of picking up my pipe or my fork. Or else it is the fork which now has a certain way of getting itself picked up, I don't know. Just now, when I was on the point of coming into my room, I stopped short because I felt in my hand a cold object which attracted my attention by means of a sort of personality. I opened my hand and looked: I was simply holding the doorknob. This morning, at the library, when the Autodidact came to say good-morning to me, it took me ten seconds to recognize him. I saw an unknown face which was barely a face. And then there was his hand, like a fat maggot in my hand.
>
> In the streets too there are a great many suspicious noises to be heard.

The narrator goes on to question what exactly has changed. Is it his environment or is it himself?

He seems, to me, to be describing a state of mind which is not an everyday one, and is not a mystical one, but which may well be an abnormal one. He may, in fact, be describing derealization. When this is present the world appears less real than it usually does and meaning drains away from things. The narrator in Sartre's novel does not know what his fingers are holding when they close on a doorknob. It takes ten seconds for a face to be recognized.

He seems to use the word 'nausea' metaphorically, in an attempt to describe these experiences. He is not sure whether the change is in the world around him or in himself. He thus raises, also, the possibility of depersonalization; and indeed, these two, derealization and depersonalization, often occur together.

Note also that he complains that 'in the streets too there are a great many suspicious noises to be heard'. The actual meaning of things is less certain, but possible meanings are more numerous. His world is strange, weird, uncanny, eerie.

Consider, for a moment, a person looking at a rose. In ordinary life, especially at the Average State **A**, which I suppose to be the most balanced and ordinary place of all, we are unlikely to actually make the following response; but if asked, we would probably agree that:

'A rose is a rose.'

In a Mystical State at **M** we might agree with Gertrude Stein, that:

'A rose is a rose is a rose.'

But, in the uncanny world of derealization and depersonalization we might assert, with hesitation:

'I *think* this is a rose.'

Only, however, to follow with the question:

'Or is it?'

I place this state at a place of low intensity which I call the Eerie State, or **Ee** for short. See Figures 12.4 and 12.9.

My argument is that when intensity drops below the Average level at **A**, a person feels strange and full of uncertainty. Things lose their usual significance and acquire too many *possible* meanings.

The security of everyday life has been lost. This is the land of the ghost story, where things may not be what they seem, the world of Edgar Allan Poe (1927) and of Walter de la Mare (1979).

Sartre calls this feeling 'a sort of nausea'. He struggles to express it. It is clearly *partially* ineffable. Yet he manages to convey something of the quality of this state.

I call this type of ineffability Type II. This is the type associated with an abnormally low intensity, at **Ee**.

Moreover, although in Section 12.1 of Chapter 12 I have put

an arrow from **Ee** to **Z**, I cannot find any clear descriptions of the Zero State, **Z**. I think this is because, at **Z**, words have completely lost their meanings, e.g. the 'word salads' of the catatonic schizophrenic who, I speculate, may sometimes be at **Z**. Thus the ineffability at **Z** may be the limiting case of the ineffability at **Ee**. Both would then belong to my Type II of ineffability.

I would like to compare the limiting case of Type I, at **V**, where the *person* disappears, with the limiting case of Type II, at **Z**, where *meaning* disappears. **V** and **Z** are at the extreme points on the intensity scale and, at both, ineffability is complete.

These ideas about ineffability are discussed at length in Chapter 12.

6.4 The doctor–patient relationship in treatment

The descriptions of treatment given above omit to mention the human relationship between the doctor and patient which is an important factor in treatment. It is well brought out in Stafford-Clark and Smith's (1980) textbook.

The effect upon a patient, when it is lacking, is described by Sutherland (1976) in his brilliant description of his own *Breakdown*, and eventual recovery.

6.5 The possible use of computer graphics

The illnesses portrayed above are very sketchily described. To fill out these sketches it would be necessary to show a person moving, through night and day, for a period long enough to allow the characteristic patterns of the illness to display themselves.

Appendix I is a program which generates computer graphics of the *map* and places the representative point at various places upon them. This approach, if extended, would allow the characteristic sequences of states of the different illnesses to be compared.

6.6 Chapter summary

Symptoms and signs are defined. A warning is given against self-diagnosis. Some typical mental illnesses are described, including a depressive illness, mania and schizophrenia. To plot them on the *map* requires the use of extra variables, such as anxiety.

Depersonalization and derealization are briefly discussed and illustrated by a text from Sartre's novel *Nausea*. This leads on to the suggestion that the limiting kind of depersonalization and derealization might be catatonic states, such as occur in schizophrenia.

Ineffability Type II is defined, a topic which will be taken up again later in Chapter 12, in relation to three other Types.

The importance of the human relationship between the doctor and the patient is emphasized.

The possible use of computer graphics is discussed.

Chapter 7

Plotting the effects of drugs

This Chapter relies heavily on the book written for the general reader on the psychoactive drugs, i.e. drugs which alter mood or behaviour, by Julien (1978).

Man has long sought to produce in himself various kinds of drug-induced states of mind. Some drugs are familiar to us in everyday life, such as caffeine, nicotine and alcohol. The dangers of drugs have also been long-known, especially those of physical and psychological dependence. Moreover, whereas many drugs are used in the treatment of mental illnesses, some drugs can themselves cause mental illnesses.

In this Chapter I will briefly describe a few of the features of the following drugs: phenobarbitone, amphetamine, amytriptiline, lithium carbonate, chlorpromazine and lysergic acid diethylamide (LSD). The above selection has several important omissions. In particular I have not discussed the opiates such as morphine.

7.1 Some typical drugs

Phenobarbitone

This drug belongs to the wide group of drugs called the sedative-hypnotics (a hypnotic is a sleep-inducing drug), which includes alcohol and anti-anxiety drugs such as chlordiazepoxide and diazepam.

Phenobarbitone – like the other members of this group – causes, depending on the dose: relief from anxiety, excitation (depending on mood and personality), sedation, sleep, anaesthesia, coma and eventually, death.

Starting from the various phases of ordinary healthy states

of mind shown in Figure 4.2 we can consider in turn how to plot the sequence of effects due to phenobarbitone. The sedative effect is shown in Figure 7.1. If the dose is increased until coma is reached the representative point of the person must be shown at the Origin O, as in Figure 7.2. No other information about the mental state can be shown on the *map*.

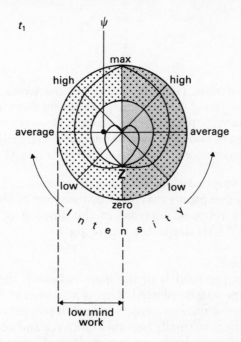

Figure 7.1 A sedated person. Main variables: mind work – low; mood – pleasant; concentration – reduced, but still in concentrated zone; intensity – average. Extra variable: loss of anxiety if previously present

Using the paper models of the *map* which constitute Appendix II it is now possible to trace some of the intermediate stages between Figures 7.1 and 7.2. In particular a stage of excitement may occur with phenobarbitone, as with alcohol, and according to the person's personality the mood may be pleasant, or unpleasant and aggressive.

Phenobarbitone is restricted nowadays to the treatment of epilepsy because it causes physical and psychological depend-

120   *Using the* map *to plot mental states*

O

Figure 7.2 In a coma. The main variables are indeterminate apart
from mind work. Nothing can be said about intensity,
mood, or the concentration ratio. However, mind work
can be said to be zero. The *map* of the mental state can
therefore only be shown as its own Origin, **O**

ence. If it is stopped after being used for some time, among the
withdrawal symptoms may be a disturbance of sleep associated with a rebound increase in the amount of rapid eye
movement (REM) sleep. (See Figure 4.4.)

Amphetamine
Using the paper models of the *map* as before, the effects of
amphetamine can be plotted. This is a stimulant drug which
causes alertness and counteracts fatigue. It prevents sleep and a
person taking it normally becomes talkative and active.

Prolonged use leads to psychological dependence. A
psychotic illness closely resembling schizophrenia can occur,
especially after prolonged high dosage. There are delusions of
persecution and hallucinations, but these are reversible if the
drug is withdrawn.

An anti-depressant drug: amitryptiline
Consider a person suffering from a depressive illness, as
discussed in Chapter 6 (see Figure 6.1). Many such people can
be helped by one of the anti-depressant drugs, such as amitryptiline, which tend to reduce the intensity of general mood, to
change the latter from unpleasant to pleasant, and to remove
any delusions, if present.

An anti-manic drug: lithium carbonate

Lithium carbonate is used to treat manic states (see Figure 6.2). It can also be given on a long-term basis to prevent such attacks occurring or to prevent recurrent depressive illnesses occurring, or both (however, it does not itself cure a particular attack of depressive illness once it has started). Lithium carbonate, when successful in the treatment of mania, gradually reduces the mind work, improves concentration, reduces intensity and removes extra symptoms such as delusions, hallucinations and anxiety, if present.

An antipsychotic drug: chlorpromazine

This drug – together with many related drugs similar to it in effect – has had a major effect on the behaviour and experience of people suffering from schizophrenia (see Figure 6.5). It reduces or removes hallucinations and delusions, calms excitement, removes anxiety and reduces 'thought disorder'.

A psychedelic drug: LSD

Lysergic acid diethylamide (LSD) is a psychedelic drug, i.e. a mind-expanding or mind-revealing drug (see Hoffer and Osmond, 1967; Julien, 1978; Slater and Roth, 1977).

Starting with a healthy, concentrated, waking state, the effects of LSD are to cause a sequence of rapid fluctuations in general mood and intensity. The general mood changes from pleasant to unpleasant, and vice versa. The intensity changes from high, giving euphoria or terrifying dark states, to low, giving depersonalized states, either pleasant or unpleasant.

There may be anxiety or acute fear, amounting to panic. The person may become restless and aggressive, or may perform dangerous actions.

Although true hallucinations probably do not occur – in the sense of experiences not due to actual objects in the environment – nevertheless perception is highly distorted in characteristic ways. Cobweb patterns are often seen over things, including faces. Colours seem far more intense than usual, or even to be colours never seen before. People and things change, faces become evil grinning masks, and so on. Some of these changes are represented in Figure 7.3.

These fluctuating effects can continue for many hours and

Figure 7.3 The effects of LSD

(a) Euphoric state. Main variables: mind work – high; intensity – between average and high; concentration – relatively low; mood – pleasant. Extra variables: giggling and laughing; visual hyperaesthesia; illusions; hallucinations, sometimes; delusions, sometimes;

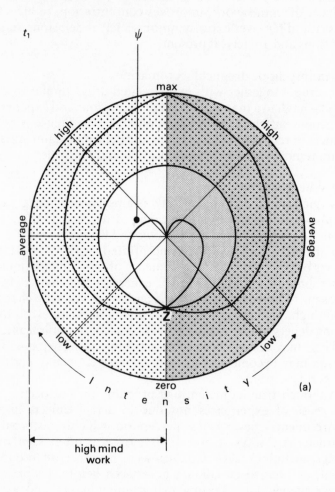

(a)

alterations to time sense; sense of mystical significance.
See Slater and Roth (1977), Julien (1978) and Jaspers
(1913).
(b) Dark and anxious state. This is the dark equivalent of
the state described in (a). It can be a horrific experience,
the 'hell' corresponding to the 'heaven' described in (a)

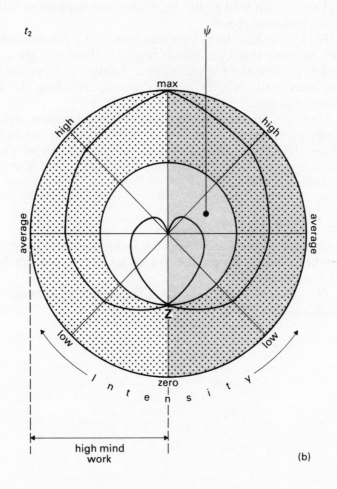

(b)

are sometimes described as returning months later, as 'flash-backs'.

Although sometimes called the 'hallucinogenic' drugs, the term psychedelic, meaning mind-expanding or mind-manifesting, is better, since, as mentioned above, the distortions of perception which occur are not true hallucinations. They are accompanied by delusions which may be paranoid, and which can lead to the aggressive and dangerous actions also mentioned above.

The psychedelic drugs have also been called 'psychotomimetic', meaning that their effects resemble those of a psychosis and, in particular, of schizophrenia. Another comparison that has been made is with mystical states, including the dark mystical states.

There are, understandably, resemblances between mystical states, some mental illnesses and the effects of the psychedelic drugs. There are also, however, differences. These resemblances occur in the border-zones discussed in Chapter 4, Sections 4.1 and 4.2.

7.2 Chapter summary

Some typical drugs are discussed, including phenobarbitone, amphetamine, amitriptyline and LSD. Other important drugs are mentioned.

The similarities between drug states, mental illnesses and mystical states are discussed briefly.

PART FOUR

Other interpretations

This part of the book explores two other ways in which the *map* can be 'interpreted': first, in Chapter 8, the *map* is used as a framework for considering mythological ideas. Then, in Chapter 9, a set of tables is presented, naming works of art which seem to me to express some of the mental states on the *map*.

Chapter 8

Mythology

In this chapter I take a few of the characters from ancient Greek mythology and relate them to the *map*. Then I discuss creation myths.

8.1 The nature of myths

Myths are stories about gods or heroes. They are usually regarded as works of fiction. However, Jung (1952) took a different view, as follows:

> Myth is not fiction: it consists of facts that are continually repeated and can be observed over and over again. It is something that happens to man, and men have mythical fates just as much as the Greek heroes do.

Seen this way we can regard myths as 'models' of our experience and behaviour, both when we are alone and when we interact with other people or with nature. Myths, then, are patterns or examples. They show what can happen to each one of us.

They are not used in the same way as scientific models. We do not test myths scientifically. We just 'try them on for size', matching them to our life until we find one that fits and which seems to help us to understand what is happening or even to plan what to do next.

All religions have a collection of stories, and these stories – Christian parables, Hasidic stories, Sufi stories, Zen stories and so on – are used like myths in the above sense, as patterns and examples.

It is perhaps in the nature of myths that the best accounts of

them are obtained from authors capable of creating a myth or
two themselves. I have gone, therefore, to the work of Robert
Graves (1955), James Branch Cabell (1919), Saki (1911) and
Kenneth Grahame (1908) for my information.

8.2 Some of the Greek gods and heroes

Greek mythology is a labyrinth and I have only explored a few
corners of it, baffled by the elusive figures that appear and
disappear.

However, I have picked out a few of the main gods of
ancient Greece, and I suggest that their qualities link some of
them to particular mental states – places which can be shown
on the *map* – and others to the movements between mental
states, to particular journeys.

After all, these are not new ideas. The gods and goddesses of
old have always been seen, by some people, to be guardians of
certain places. They have also been seen as forces which move
us, divine forces which sway us mere mortals, propelling us
from one place to another. These forces operate upon a person
to make him change his mental state. The gods can thus be seen
sometimes as states and at other times as operators. See Figure
8.1.

Let us look, therefore, at some of the Greek gods whose lairs
or palaces, or pathways, can be plotted on the *map*.

Zeus

The entire *map* belongs to Zeus, as he is the most powerful of
the gods, the father of the gods and of men. But see Chaos,
below, for the region that lies off the *map*, beyond the Origin.

Pan

I will continue with the god of nature, the great god Pan, or as
Cabell (1919), calls him, 'The Brown Man with Queer Feet'. I
locate Pan at point Z, the Z-state, of zero intensity.

Jurgen, the hero of Cabell's novel of that name, found Pan in
a clearing in the Druid Forest. This clearing seems to tally fairly
well with the Z-state. Druids undoubtedly occupy an uncanny
corner of the *map* and the Z-state is at the limit of the uncanny.
Jurgen calls Pan 'Lord of the Two Truths', but we are not
informed what they are. However, two of my equations, since

they each apply to a pair of opposites and hence appear literally nonsensical, might qualify. They are as follows:

(1) **Z**, the Zero State = intensity zero

applied to both the light and the dark sides of the *map*;

(2) **Z**, the Zero State is where the concentration ratio = 1

applied to both the concentrated and the diffuse zones.

Pan tells Jurgen that he, Pan, 'is everything that was and that is to be'. He also asserts that 'Never has any mortal been able to discover what I am.' These statements fit the idea that the mind has its Origin **O**, which lies in the mysterious plane of The

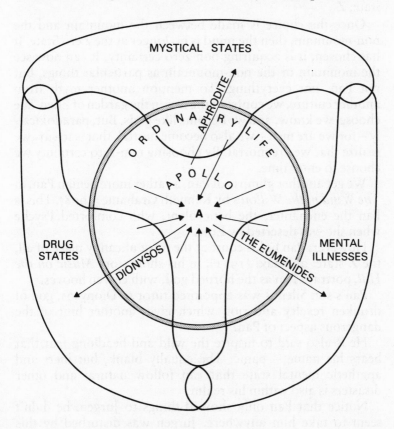

Figure 8.1 The gods as operators

Void **V**, the Zero State **Z**, and **#MAX**, diffuse **MAX** the point of maximal diffusion.

They must apply to all things also, since minds are made from things, or, alternatively, things are what are to be found on minds – all minds – past, present and future.

As to what Pan is now, no mind can hope to know that, because nothing, no-thing, no one particular thing nor even many things, nor even the idea of Pan himself, can be grasped when the mind has access to all things, i.e. when it has access to all potential things, such as the mountain and the non-mountain, seen at once. Each is potentially present – all potential things – held at zero intensity of certainty, at the Zero State, **Z**.

Once the choice is made between the mountain and the non-mountain, then the mind is no longer at the Zero State. It has chosen, it is acquiring non-zero certainty. It can now see the mountain or the non-mountain as particular things, but not Pan, not everything. To mention another myth from another culture, we confront the tree in the garden of Eden. We choose, we know, and we become like gods. But, paradoxically – for we are men – we also become mortal, that is to say, we realize that we are mortal. By choosing non-zero certainty we choose to enter time.

We get another glimpse of Pan, a rather more benign Pan, in *The Wind in the Willows* by Kenneth Grahame (1908). This is Pan the enchanter, the benevolent, who comforted Psyche when she was deserted by Eros.

However, Pan holds court at the most uncanny place of all, the Z-state, and Saki (1911), in his short story *Music on the Hill*, portrays Pan as the horned god, with cloven hooves.

Pan's son Silenus was appointed tutor to Dionysos, god of drunken revelry and riot, which gives another hint of the dangerous aspect of Pan.

He is also said to inspire the wild and headlong fear that bears his name – panic. The equally blank, but inert and apathetic mental state that can follow natural and other disasters is also within his realm.

Notice that Pan only showed things to Jurgen, he didn't seem to take him anywhere. Jurgen was disturbed by this meeting, but not changed by it. I interpret this as the journey:

A ⇌ Z

Jurgen bounces back off the **Z**-state. This is consistent with Figure 8.2. Contrast the arrows at **V** where only a person passing through **V** from **M** or **– M** can touch **V**.

Pan presides over the place of Zero Certainty and is himself called 'All'. At the **Z**-state all things are potential but none are certain.

Pan lives at the **Z**-point, which is Nature, the birthplace of All Things. It is a source or spring, a 'fount' welling up from the 'Origin' beneath, at **O**.

Apollo
The god Apollo stands for moderation, for the middle way, for the golden mean, for life graced by music and the other arts.

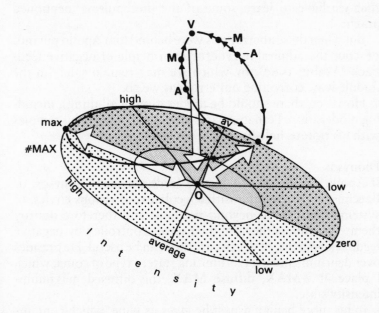

Figure 8.2 Pathways through **V, O, Z** and **#MAX** (diffuse **MAX**)

We need his wisdom. He advises us to take holidays and not to overwork. He helps us to overcome illness, and Asklepios, the great healer, was his son. See Figure 8.1.

Apollo shared for a year the life of men, and so knows what is good for them, especially **A**, the **A**-state, the Golden **A**-state. He presides over all the mental and physical control mechanisms, the blessed homeostats, that keep us there at the **A**-state for so much of our time. Apollo's main work is done 'by the light of day' and he keeps us balanced and sane. He propels us back to **A**, to the Golden Average State, in between our excursions into sleep or daydreams or places further afield.

Although Apollo is the god of moderation, of 'know thyself', and of the golden mean, he did not achieve this balanced state at once. Before doing so he fell into error and was duly punished. He took his punishment meekly, while at the same time not overlooking the chances of self-improvement available to him. He was sent to a sort of open prison where he made himself useful to the governor. This episode reminds us that we have to learn some of the mechanisms mentioned above.

But when these aberrations were behind him Apollo put into practice the admirable cybernetic principle of negative feedback (Ashby, 1960), by which we may remain safely in the middle way, correcting our errors as we go.

However, there should be moderation in all things, including moderation. Perhaps that is why Apollo shares his temples with his riotous half-brother, Dionysos.

Dionysos
If Apollo is the god of negative feedback then Dionysos, or Bacchus, is the god of positive feedback, of vicious circles, of systems that can go beyond the limit and therefore destroy themselves unless they are themselves controlled by negative feedback systems, in which case they can be useful. He presides over delirium, and over its limiting state, a type of coma, which I place at #**MAX**, diffuse **MAX**, the diffused maximum-intensity state.

In his more benign aspect he gives us wine, which contains one of our most familiar operators, alcohol. A few drinks in good company will often take us from **A** to a place of heightened experience, rosy but slightly unreal, a place on the way towards a Peak Experience at **P**, but less intense.

Chaos
In the centre of the *map* is the Origin, **O**, one of whose doors is the formless Void at **V**. Here Chaos reigns, firstborn of all the gods: 'A gaping void, a yawning gulf, a chasm or abyss' (Little, Fowler and Coulson, 1962).

The Origin is not on the *map*. To say where the Origin lies would be to describe a world beyond our mind, for the Origin **O** is one of the limits of the mind.

Hades
Beyond the Origin is, I suppose, the dark kingdom of Hades, Lord of the dead. Not even Orpheus, a hero, could bring Eurydice back, from here, alive.

Aphrodite
The goddess of erotic passion, Aphrodite, is, like Dionysos, quite an operator. She moves us around on the *map* in sudden jumps that can take us unawares: from the **A**-state to a blissful **P**-state or equally, when unrequited, to the agonising −**P**-state. W. H. Auden called her 'anarchic', but it is her son, Eros, the blindfold marksman, who shoots at random on her behalf.

Odysseus and Psyche
Man himself is represented on the *map* by Odysseus, the voyager, who was, by descent, only partly divine. I use the Greek letter psi, ψ, to mark the representative point of any person, including Odysseus, on my *map* as he navigates his inner space. This letter stands for Psyche, by which I denote our individuality.

Hermes
Let us conclude with the trickster-god, Hermes (or Mercury). He is a bit of a joker but always the gentleman, and he has lovely manners. After all, he needs them at the Olympian Foreign Office. He tells us a few white lies as a negotiator but then, he always puts things tactfully.

He also runs the Celestial Post Office. But he never tampers with the mail even though information is his stock-in-trade. He is, naturally, taking a keen interest in computers these days.

He is associated with the Egyptian god Thoth and hence with enlightenment, that secret journey from **A** to **A*** that is so hard to describe.

8.3 Creation myths

Something from Nothing
A creation myth tries to explain how something – our world – arose out of nothing. Or, at least, out of nothing that is inside our world.

So a creation myth has the form

No-thing ⟶ Some-thing
or Super-natural ⟶ Natural
or Creator ⟶ Creation

There is usually a symmetrical myth, based on mysticism, in which the natural world returns to its origin.

No-thing ⟵ Some-thing

The complete mystical path is then a journey in both directions, thus:

(1) The mystic is born and grows up:

No-thing ⟶ Some-thing

(2) The mystic returns to The Void

Nothing ⟵ Some-thing

(3) The mystic is 're-born', enlightened

No-thing ⟶ Some-thing*

We can put the two directions together, thus:

$$\text{No-thing} \underset{\text{once}}{\overset{\text{twice}}{\rightleftarrows}} \text{Some-thing (or Some-thing*)}$$

The pairs of opposites

When something is studied it is always possible to see its complement. Look at a mountain and you can also see the non-mountain, as shown in Figure 8.3.

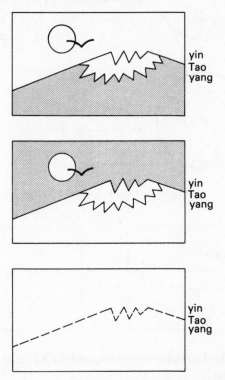

Figure 8.3 The mountain and the non-mountain

The pairs of opposites are called Yin and Yang in China and their relationship is the Tao, meaning 'The Way'. This relationship is represented in Figure 8.4.

When the pairs of opposites can be seen then the Tao is seen – in this example as the line where they join. When the pairs of opposites cannot be seen, the Tao, likewise, cannot be seen. But we can imagine it, as shown in Figure 8.5.

We are back to our basic form again, with an arrow for the Creation of something – in this case the pairs of opposites, Yin and Yang – out of nothing, and an arrow for the disappearance

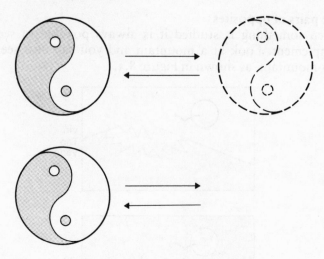

Figure 8.4 Tao, Yin and Yang

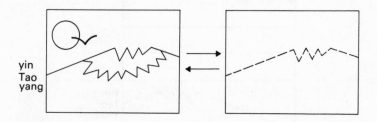

yin
Tao
yang

Figure 8.5 The Tao that can be seen, and the Tao that cannot be
　　　　seen

of the pairs of opposites and with them, apparently, the Tao
which now can no longer be seen.

We can now show the same form in other ways, as in Figure
8.6.

The creation myth in the *Tao Te Ching*

The *Tao Te Ching* by Lao Tzu (Blakney, 1955) contains a
creation myth which can be summarized as follows. The Tao
is called the secret and Yin and Yang its containers. See
Figure 8.7.

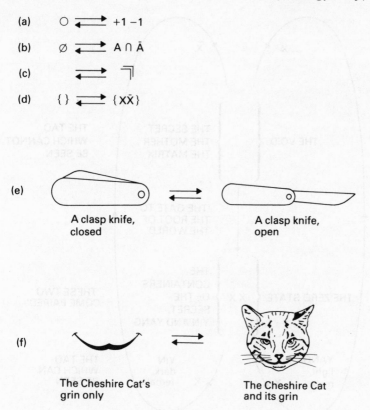

Figure 8.6 Showing the Tao

The creation myth in C. G. Jung's (c.1916) *Septem Sermones ad Mortuos*

This interesting book was written by Jung under the name of Basilides, a gnostic writer. He wrote it at a turning-point in his life, as described in his autobiography (Jung, 1961). It can be partly analysed along similar lines to the analysis of the *Tao Te Ching*, in Figure 8.7.

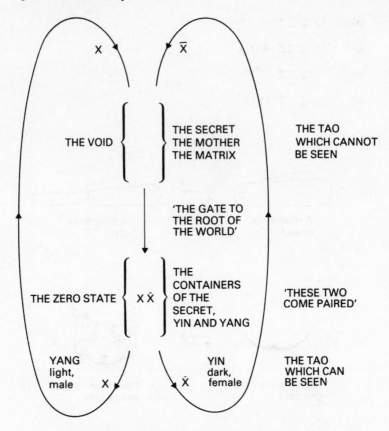

Figure 8.7 'Things have a mother' (*Tao Te Ching*)

8.4. Chapter summary

The nature of myths is discussed. Some of the Greek gods and goddesses are related to the *map*, either by being associated with places on the *map* or by being regarded as operators. An operator is a force which moves us around the *map*.

Creation myths are briefly analysed and seen to be complementary to the mystical path. The creation myth in the *Tao Te Ching* is summarized. A pseudo-gnostic book, by Jung, which contains a creation myth is also mentioned.

Chapter 9

The arts used to describe mental states

The different arts often seem to describe, illustrate, symbolize or merely hint at states of mind, including some very elusive ones. In this chapter, therefore, I have drawn up Tables which contain examples chosen from six arts – music, painting, architecture, literature, cinema and landscape – in order to convey more precisely what I mean by some of the places on the *map*.

9.1 Notes on the Tables

In these Tables I have tried, systematically, to convey my own ideas about states of mind, using these six different arts. Some readers may prefer to look first at the Table relating to the art with which they feel most 'at home', because of their personal preference – the Table for music, say.

Readers may also like to find a particular state of mind in a favourite art and then look across the other Tables to the same state in other arts. Perhaps this could turn into *The Glass Bead Game* (Hesse, 1943)?

Notation
The symbols for the various mental states (A, Ee, −Ee and so on) have been discussed previously or will be in Section 12.1 of Chapter 12. Where I use the letter X it indicates several different mental states, all with the same general form. Thus (X) stands for dreaming states in general. Such states could be of high, average or low intensity.

The Void is not a state in which a person can stay for a period of clock time. It is at the limit of the intensity dimension and takes part in the changes indicated in Figure 9.1. So descriptions of V always involve a change of state in progress.

At the limit, V and Z are identified with the Origin, O, to which they are like the front and back doors respectively. I think it is possible to stay for a while at Z as well as at the Origin, O. However, the Origin itself is not included in the Tables.

Selection
The examples I have chosen for the Tables are a personal selection and I make no great claims for them. I could have chosen other examples and readers will be able to make their own personal Tables.

I am really trying to make the general point that we can, and

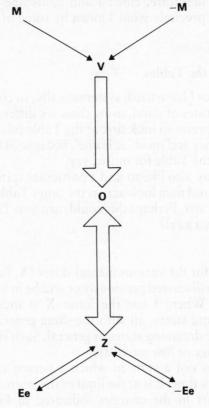

Figure 9.1 The Void, V, as a point of change

do, use the arts very widely, in order to express our states of mind in all their subtlety.

Also, I do not wish to give a false impression of erudition. For example, I have chosen Haydn's 'London' symphony to stand for **A**, the 'average state', because I think it does so very well, but it should not be assumed that I know any other Haydn symphonies. In all the Tables my selection has just been made from what I happen to know.

Only one or two of my examples are rather obscure, e.g. the film *Rain*, directed by Joris Ivens. I saw it at the film club at my school. It shows rain falling in a town – Amsterdam perhaps? – and making continually changing patterns in puddles and down window-panes.

Most of my examples are, however, either well-known or easily referred to in art books and paperbacks. My own particular choices are not important. As I said above, what I wish to convey is the very idea that such choices can provide a common language by means of which we can communicate to each other very elusive states of mind, and do so with some precision.

The six tables form a larger Table if they are placed side by side, so that one can use a knowledge of one art to gain entry to another, with mental states as the key.

Omissions

Several states, on the *map* have not been included in these Tables. The Origin **O**, itself, is omitted, although some modern works of art have perhaps described it. However, it could be considered to be not so much on the *map* as where the *map* 'is at', as they say in America. Also omitted are Delirium, #**High**, Dark Delirium, −#**High**, the Dark Outsider States, −|**X**|, and the Attached States, |**X**|. I have also omitted 'extra variables' such as anxiety, phobias, compulsions and so on.

These Tables could possibly be extended so as to include other states, and 'extra variables'. However, this method of tabulation might lose its usefulness if one tried to push it too far, in an effort to discriminate between very similar states of mind.

Here then, are the six Tables, dealing with music, painting, architecture, literature, cinema and landscape.

Table 9.1 Places on the *map* in music

State	Symbol	Example
The Void	V	Oliver Messiaen: *L'Ascension*
Mystical State Proper	M	Frederick Delius: *The Mass of Life*
Dark Mystical State Proper	−M	Sir Edward Elgar: *The Dream of Gerontius*
Peak Experience	P	Richard Strauss: Opera, *Capriccio*
Dark Peak Experience	−P	Benjamin Britten: *War Requiem*
Average State	A	Joseph Haydn: Symphony No. 104, 'The London'
Dark Average State	−A	Ludwig van Beethoven: Piano Sonata Op. 81a, 'Les Adieux'
Eerie State	Ee	Wolfgang Amadeus Mozart: Piano Concerto, K482
Dark Eerie State	−Ee	Wolfgang Amadeus Mozart: Symphony No. 41, K551, 'The Jupiter'
Zero State	Z	Ludwig van Beethoven: Symphony No. 9 (First Movement)
Daydreaming State	#A	Claude Debussy: *L'Après-midi d'un faune*
Dreaming States	(X)	Béla Bartók: Piano Concerto No. 3
Dark Dreaming States	(−X)	Dimitri Shostakovich: Symphony No. 13
Outsider States	¦X¦	Bohuslav Martinu: Concerto for Two String Orchestras, Piano and Timpani
Enlightened States	X*	Christoph Willibald Gluck: Opera, *Orpheus and Euridice*

Table 9.2 Places on the *map* in painting
(A typical painting has been mentioned, for each artist)

State	Symbol	Example
The Void	**V**	Joseph Mallord William Turner: *Snowstorm: Steamboat off a Harbour Mouth*
Mystical State Proper	**M**	William Blake: *The Angels Appearing to the Shepherds*
Dark Mystical State Proper	**−M**	Francis Bacon: *Head II, 1949*
Peak Experience	**P**	Samuel Palmer: *The Magic Apple-Tree*
Dark Peak Experience	**−P**	Vincent van Gogh: *Old Man in Sorrow*
Average State	**A**	Walter Richard Sickert: *Old Bedford*
Dark Average State	**−A**	Lucien Freud: *Cock's Head*
Eerie State	**Ee**	Ivon Hitchens: *Dark Pool, 1960*
Dark Eerie State	**−Ee**	James Ensor: *Masks Confronting Death*
Zero State	**Z**	Kurt Schwitters: *Merzbild Einunddreissig, 1920*
Daydreaming State	**#A**	Sir Edward Burne-Jones: *King Cophetua and the Beggar Maid*
Dreaming States	**(X)**	René Magritte: *Time Transfixed*
Dark Dreaming States	**(−X)**	Max Ernst: *The Entire City, 1934*
Outsider States	**¦X¦**	Edvard Munch: *The Cry*
Enlightened States	**X***	Paul Cézanne: *Sainte-Victoire, 1905–6*

Table 9.3 Places on the *map* in architecture

State	Symbol	Example
The Void	V	Gustave Eiffel: The Eiffel Tower, Paris
Mystical State Proper	M	Philip Hardwick: The Euston Arch, London (demolished)
Dark Mystical State Proper	−M	G.-B. Piranesi: *The Prisons* Etchings
Peak Experience	P	John Nash: The Royal Pavilion, Brighton
Dark Peak Experience	−P	Sir Charles Barry: Pentonville Prison, London
Average State	A	Andrea Palladio: Villa Rotonda, Vicenza
Dark Average State	−A	Mazes
Eerie State	Ee	Sir John Soane: The Bank of England, London (what's left of it)
Dark Eerie State	−Ee	George Dance: Old Newgate Prison, London (demolished)
Zero State	Z	Sandcastles
Daydreaming State	#A	Summer-houses
Dreaming States	(X)	Sir Alfred Gilbert, The Alexandra Memorial, Marlborough Gate, London
Dark Dreaming States	(−X)	Highgate Cemetery, London
Outsider States	¦X¦	Caravans
Enlightened States	X*	Michaelangelo: Vestibule of the Laurentian Library, Florence

Table 9.4 Places on the *map* in literature
(In English or in English translation)

State	Symbol	Example
The Void	V	Abu Hamid al-Ghazali: *Mishkat al-Anwar*
Mystical State Proper	M	Saint Teresa of Ávila: *The 'Life'*
Dark Mystical State Proper	−M	Saint John of the Cross: *The Dark Night of the Soul*
Peak Experience	P	D. H. Lawrence: *Women in Love* (Chapter 1)
Dark Peak Experience	−P	William Shakespeare: *Macbeth*
Average State	A	The daily newspaper
Dark Average State	−A	Charles Dickens: *Our Mutual Friend*
Eerie State	Ee	Robert Aickman: *Dark Entries*
Dark Eerie State	−Ee	H. H. Munro (Saki): *The Cobweb*
Zero State	Z	George Spencer Brown: *Laws of Form*
Daydreaming State	#A	Italo Calvino: *Invisible Cities*
Dreaming States	(X)	Gérard de Nerval: *Sylvie*
Dark Dreaming States	(−X)	Franz Kafka: *The Castle*
Outsider States	¦X¦	Albert Camus: *The Outsider*
Enlightened States	X*	Lao Tzu: *Tao Te Ching*

Table 9.5 Places on the *map* in cinema
(with directors' names)

State	Symbol	Example
The Void	V	Stanley Kubrick: *2001 – A Space Odyssey*
Mystical State Proper	M	Leni Riefenstahl: *The Blue Light*
Dark Mystical State Proper	−M	Carol Read: *The Third Man*
Peak Experience	P	Jean Renoir: *Une Partie de Campagne*
Dark Peak Experience	−P	Alfred Hitchcock: *The Birds*
Average State	A	Georges Rouquier: *Farrebique*
Dark Average State	−A	Jean-Luc Godard: *Le Mépris*
Eerie State	Ee	Jean Cocteau: *Orphée*
Dark Eerie State	−Ee	Joseph Losey: *The Servant*
Zero State	Z	Joris Ivens: *Rain*
Daydreaming State	#A	Luchino Visconti: *The Leopard*
Dreaming States	(X)	Alain Resnais: *Last Year at Marienbad*
Dark Dreaming States	(−X)	Patrick McGoohan and others: TV series *The Prisoner*
Outsider States	|X|	Orson Welles: *Citizen Kane*
Enlightened States	X*	Anthony Pelissier: *The History of Mr Polly*

Table 9.6 Places on the *map* in landscape, etc.

State	Symbol	Example
The Void	V	The Sea
Mystical State Proper	M	The Cascade at Chatsworth House, Derbyshire
Dark Mystical State Proper	−M	Seaton Delaval
Peak Experience	P	The Herbaceous Border at Hampton Court, near London
Dark Peak Experience	−P	Hot sulphurous springs in Iceland
Average State	A	Any market place
Dark Average State	−A	Bus shelters in winter
Eerie State	Ee	Wasdale, in the Lake District
Dark Eerie State	−Ee	The vicinity of Nottingham Castle
Zero State	Z	Fog
Daydreaming State	#A	Sandpits
Dreaming States	(X)	A distant prospect of San Gimignano, Italy
Dark Dreaming States	(−X)	Clover-leaf junctions on motorways
Outsider States	|X|	The area behind St Pancras Station, London
Enlightened States	X*	Cambridge

9.2 Chapter summary

The different arts can be used to describe or illustrate different states of mind. A set of six Tables are drawn up. Music, painting, architecture, literature, cinema and landscape each provide examples relating to a set of fifteen states of mind.

PART FIVE

Evolution of
the *map*

This part of the book traces the evolution of the *map*. First, in Chapter 10, it places the *map* in the context of other psychological maps, not all of which, however, are maps of mental states. Then, in Chapter 11, it shows how the present *map* gradually developed over a considerable time, by way of being a two-dimensional map, and then a box-like three-dimensional one. This in turn went through a dramatic change in shape which led to the present *map*.

Chapter 10

Other psychological maps

In this Chapter I describe, first, some other maps of mental states, each of which has one or more features resembling the present *map*.

Then I mention another set of maps of mental states which do not resemble the present *map*.

Lastly, I present some other maps which display psychological features other than mental states. However, some of these include mental states as well.

I have interpreted the word 'map' very widely in this chapter, so as to include a variety of schemes and diagrams.

10.1 Maps of mental states with some resemblance to the present *map*

The Wheel of Life

The Buddhist Wheel of Life, or *Bhavachakra*, presents a set of scenarios, including heaven, hell, a land of animals, a land of humans, a land of titans (*asuras*) and a land of ghosts (*pretas*). These scenarios, or 'states of existence', occupy segments of the wheel.

Figure 10.1 is modified from a book by Blofeld (1970). It is the key to an illustration of the Wheel of Life in the same book. The similarity of my *map* to this is obvious.

The inner hub, labelled *abc* contains the three 'fires of evil' which keep the Wheel turning – craving, wrath and ignorance. The sections marked *d* show happy people on the left, 'on the way up', and miserable people on the right, 'on the way down'. The rim shows the 'chain of causality'.

The whole Wheel is in the grip of the demon Yama, *g*, who represents *avidhya* or delusion.

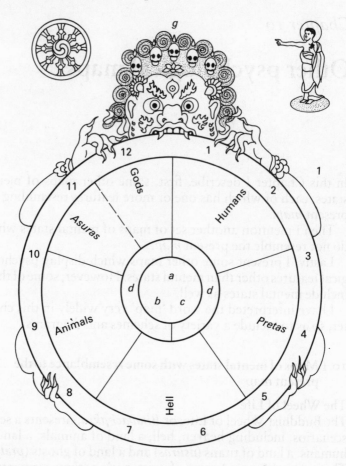

Figure 10.1 The Wheel of Life (from Blofeld, 1970)

Fischer's map

Figure 10.2 shows the map devised by Fischer (1975). It has a circular scale on which several different variables are placed. Various aspects of meditation, mystical states and mental illnesses are also shown. This map relates mental states to the neurophysiological theory that there is an ergotropic system and a complementary trophotropic system in the brain.

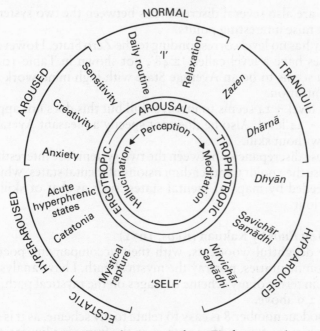

Figure 10.2 Fischer's map (from Fischer, 1975)

Lilly's levels of consciousness

Lilly (1973) has produced a set of levels of consciousness to which he has assigned numbers. This system shows a close correspondence with some of the mental states of my own *map*. See Table 10.1.

Table 10.1 Lilly's levels of consciousness compared with places on the present *map*

Lilly's level	Present map	Lilly's level	Present map
+ 3	Mystical State Proper to The Void	− 3	Dark Mystical State Proper to The Void
+ 6	Mystical State Proper	− 6	Dark Mystical State Proper
+12	Peak Experience	−12	Dark Peak Experience
+24	Average State (using a skill)	−24	Dark Average State

There are also several discrepancies between the two systems which raise interesting points.

Lilly has no level corresponding to the Zero State. However, he does have a level called '±48', not shown in Table 10.1, which seems to be an Average State with high mind work or concentration.

His level +24 seems to involve skill but this does not apply to his −24 level. Also he does not specify a pleasant Average State without skill.

These discrepancies between the two systems are interesting because they point to other dimensions of mental states, which are needed by maps of mental states, such as that of skilled behaviour.

The Ten Bulls by Kakuan (Reps, 1971)
These delightful woodcuts, with their accompanying poems and commentaries, portray the mystical path. I have analysed them, in terms of my scheme of stages on the mystical path, in Table 2.9 above.

Woodcut number 8 is easy to relate to my scheme, as it is an empty picture-frame. However, even the frame is a limitation. A bare page, or no page at all, would have been preferable, to convey 'undifferentiated unity'.

Pilgrim's Progress
Bunyan's (1678) *Pilgrim's Progress* contains the easily identifiable Slough of Despond, Vanity Fair and Doubting Castle, as well as the burden that the Pilgrim so longs to put down.

The hero's journey
Similar to the mystical path is the hero's journey in mythology (Campbell, 1949). These journeys sometimes include a voyage to the underworld, such as that made by Orpheus.

The arts
It is possible that some artists have set out, in the past, to describe a variety of mental states according to some scheme of their own. One gets hints of this in the *Labyrinths* of Borges (1964) and, more explicitly, in the *Invisible Cities* of Italo Calvino (1974), not to mention Shakespeare.

10.2 Other maps of the mind, which do not resemble the present *map*

Fludd's map
Robert Fludd, the alchemist, had an elaborate scheme of mental functions whose anatomical sites are based on the large fluid-filled cavities in the brain called the ventricles (see Blakemore, 1977). Fludd belongs to the Hermetic Tradition, described by Yates (1964).

Freud's map
I have based Figure 10.3 upon the text of Freud's (1926) book *The Question of Lay Analysis*, which contains a concise description of psycho-analysis in its later form. 'The Unconscious' is of course, by definition, off my *map*.

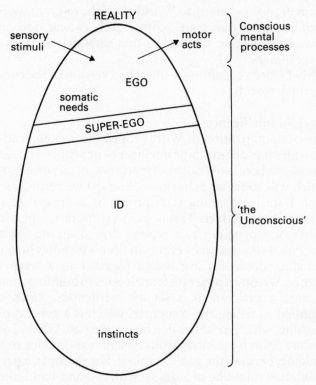

Figure 10.3 Freud's map

Catastrophe theory
There are several places on my *map* where the mental state changes very abruptly. Catastrophe theory (Zeeman, 1976) sets up models, with cusped surfaces, to account for these sorts of behaviour. Postle's (1980) entertaining book contains several relevant diagrams, notably about sleep.

Popper's Three Worlds
Sir John Eccles, in his book *The Understanding of the Brain* (1977), expounds Sir Karl Popper's concept of 'The Three Worlds'. This relates the mind (World 2) to the brain, which is part of World 1, by way of calling part of the brain the Liaison Brain. The mind–body problem is not, thereby, solved but it is, at least, focused on the brain. (See Campbell, 1970.)

World 3 is human culture as encoded into World 1. For example, books belong to World 3 and the relevant coding and decoding procedures are writing and reading. Increasingly, nowadays, the part of World 1 that embodies World 3 is that of computers.

My Figure 10.4 shows a simplified version of the concept of the three worlds.

Machine intelligence
The computerization of World 3, just mentioned, leads on to the wider topic of machine intelligence or artificial intelligence. The object here is to construct machines, or to write programs, which will simulate behaviour of a type we regard as intelligent. I am interpreting such programs as 'maps' of the behaviour they produce. This is, perhaps, more acceptable if one thinks of a program as a type of flow-diagram, for a flow-diagram is like a map of events in time – it shows how events, including decisions, are linked together in a temporal sequence. Writing a program is analogous to building a machine, because a program is a set of instructions which can be regarded as telling the computer, which is a general-purpose machine, what particular machine to be (see Ashby, 1960).

Simulation is a very rigorous type of map-making or model-building, because the goal is explicit. For example, a particular simulation might be of a device with eye-and-hand-like properties. Such a device might be required to recognize some

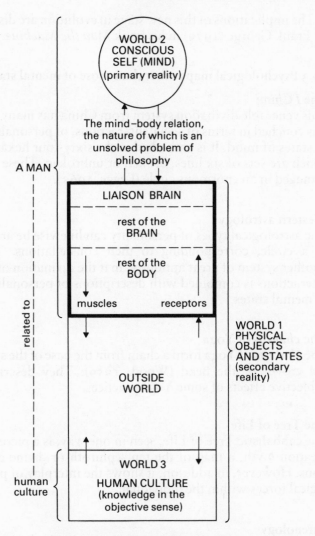

Figure 10.4 Popper's Three Worlds

particular components coming along a production line, to pick them up, to fit them together, and then to replace them on the conveyor belt. However, it should be noted that a program which is able to simulate an intelligent process is not necessarily organized in the way in which the human brain is organized.

The implications of this new stage in evolution are discussed by Frank George (1979) in his book *Man the Machine*.

10.3 Psychological maps other than those of mental states

The *I Ching*
This venerable divination system from China has many facets. It is couched in terms of social interactions, of personality and of states of mind. It is embodied in the sixty-four hexagrams, which are sets of six lines, broken or unbroken. These can be arranged in an enormous circle (Legge, 1963).

Western astrology
The astrological types of personality can likewise be arranged in a circle, corresponding to their constellations. This is another system of great antiquity. In it the divination of social interactions is combined with descriptions of personality and of mental states.

The *chakras* of Yoga
The *chakras* of Yoga form a chain from the base of the spine to the crown of the head (Wood, 1959). They describe the subjective effects of some Yoga practices.

The Tree of Life
The cabbalistic Tree of Life, seen in one way, is a picture of a creation myth, a map of the ten sephiroth or divine emanations. However, in addition, it shows the interplay of psychological forces within the individual.

Phrenology
Phrenology was the belief that the normal bumps on the human skull could yield information about the person concerned. Gradually this theory lost scientific support. However, it was a precursor of the scientific study of the effects of damage to the brain – rather than to the skull – on speech and other functions. The pioneers of these studies were Broca and Wernicke. See Blakemore (1977), mentioned above.

A Vision by W. B. Yeats

This strange book by Yeats (1937) presents a model of human personality, made up of two cones which rotate on the same axis. It has limiting points, called '1' and '15', on its angular dimension, which are interesting to compare with the limiting points on the *map*.

Jung's personality theory

Jung's book *Psychological Types* (1921) contains a theory of personality, which includes the well-known introvert–extrovert dimension.

Kurt Lewin's topological psychology

Kurt Lewin (1936) was an explicit map-maker. His maps presented social situations. To portray these he used special diagrams which showed the 'psychological space' surrounding the people involved.

Mary Douglas's grids

The grids drawn by Mary Douglas (1971), upon which she shows people moving about as they change their social relationships, are quite close to the *map*. In particular, she has very interesting things to say about the Fool and a 'Zero Point' about which he 'gyrates'.

10.4 Chapter summary

This Chapter gathers together a selection of maps (interpreting the word 'map' widely). Some of them are ancient, some are recent.

They are presented in three groups. First some maps which show resemblance to the present *map*; next, some other maps of mental states; and lastly, various maps which illustrate other psychological topics such as personality.

Chapter 11

Development of the present *map*

This chapter tells how my own *map* evolved, step by step, from the various sources described in Part One of this book. At times this evolution has been very slow, with small modifications occurring after much 'mulling-over' on my part. At other times the changes were abrupt, as when the map was box-shaped but I bent it round so that I could put the ends of the box together. Indeed, I have been working out the implications of that particular and dramatic change in the shape of the map ever since.

The present chapter is an example of the psychology of science, rather than of its philosophy. It shows how my ideas gradually evolved, helped along by the advice and criticism of the many people whom I have named, above, in my Acknowledgments.

11.1 The sequence of steps

The present *map* started to grow when I began, in about 1964, to read the mystical literature. I tried to represent the intensity of Mystical States Proper, and their dark equivalents, in relation to the number of things that the mystics described as characterizing those states. Consequently my first map looked like Figure 11.1.

The next idea I incorporated in the map was that of 'paying attention'. I noted that most mystical traditions advocated meditation, that is to say the systematic practice of concentration, of paying a lot of attention to fewer and fewer things. So I added the dimension of attention, and produced a box-shaped map as shown in Figure 11.2.

good and perspex model of this now
shape up. Happily, I did not need it (Wood
1994), for a two-dimensional one so far in this book is
concerned. But the two strands of the box-shaped map
together. The result was a sort of box, roughly with
square section .... this box ...... when locked rather
like one of those ...... which have a hole in the
cover.

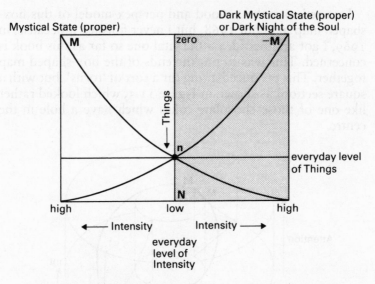

Figure 11.1 Intensity and things: a two-dimensional map

The next problem I faced was that the Mystical State proper
and the Dark Mystical State or Dark Night of the Soul on
the map ...... that it was possible to have ...... being
opposite in terms ...... of mood, one is euphoric
and the other .... they were nonetheless mapped apart
as in Figure ......

I am much aware that ...... state as it was with the
middle .... state ...... in use. The dotted area on
the ...... and .... where, finally, it would be found
the contradiction of mood .... resolved ...... resolves the
Cross see Happold 1963 ..... mapped ...... the map run, as I've
shown in Figure ......

I .... modified this, yet again ...... I did not seem
to have any particular meaning within the map it, leaving as
its only ...... the vertical line which runs inward from the
Origin O, as ......

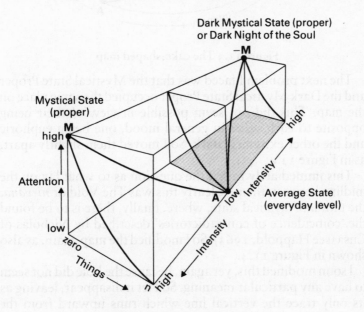

Figure 11.2 The box-shaped map

I started to make a wood and perspex model of this box-shaped map in about 1968, but I never finished it because, in 1969, I got another idea – the vital one so far as this book is concerned. This was to put the ends of the box-shaped map together. This produced a ring (or a sort of 'torus', but with a square section) as shown in Figure 11.3, which looked rather like one of those chocolate cakes which have a hole in the centre.

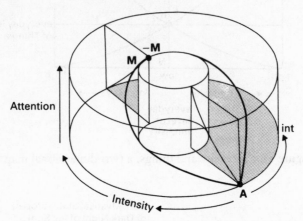

Figure 11.3 The cake-shaped map

The next problem I faced was that the Mystical State Proper and the Dark Mystical State Proper occupied the same place on the map. This did not seem possible in view of their being opposite to each other in general mood, one being euphoric and the other extremely dark. So I moved them slightly apart, as in Figure 11.4.

This immediately raised the question as to what lay on the midline between them? Clearly this was The Void or *nirvana*, the ultimate mystical state, where, finally, there is to be found the 'coincidence of contradictories' described by Nicholas of Cusa (see Happold, 1963). So I modified the map again, as also shown in Figure 11.4.

I soon modified this, yet again, because the hole did not seem to have any particular meaning. So I let it disappear, leaving as its only trace the vertical line which runs upward from the Origin, O, as shown in Figure 11.5.

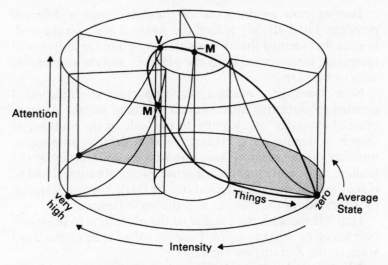

Figure 11.4 Separating the Mystical State Proper, **M**, from the Dark Mystical State Proper, −**M**, and putting in The Void, **V**

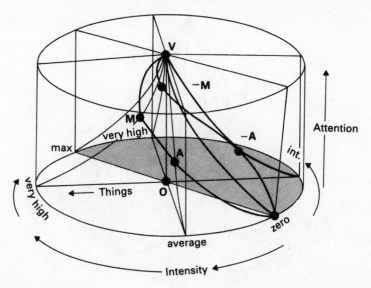

Figure 11.5 The hole disappears and the Average State, **A**, and the Dark Average State, −**A**, are placed on either side of the midline

Turning now to the front of the map I met a different problem. I had already placed the Average State on the midline, as that seemed the obvious starting-point for journeys of increasing intensity on both the pleasant and the unpleasant sides of the map.

Now, however, I made a very important modification. I decided to place this most ordinary state of all, the Average State of everyday life, slightly to one side of the midline, as shown in Figure 11.5. This gave it a definite amount of intensity on the pleasant side instead of zero intensity at the midline, which no longer made sense. Next, of course, I had to place the corresponding dark state, the Dark Average State, on the other side of the map, as also shown in Figure 11.5.

That left me with the enigma of the place at zero intensity. Not knowing what to call it I simply called it Z, or the Zero State, or the Z-state. See Figure 11.7.

A little later I extracted a cone-shaped map from inside the cake-shaped map, and I now had a map as shown in Figure

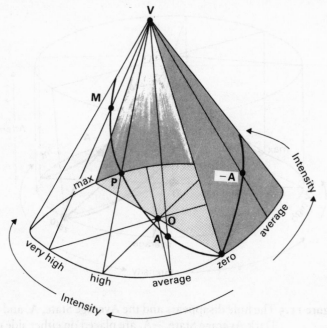

Figure 11.6 The cone-shaped map

11.6. I then found that the two curved lines which had been part of the map from the beginning (see Figures 11.1, 11.2 and 11.3) could now be drawn on the surface of the cone as a pair of spirals passing up, via **A**, to **V**.

However, it was not until 1971, and after my chapter (Clark, 1972) in Ralph Ruddock's book *Six Approaches to the Person* had gone to press, that I realized that a second pair of spirals had been waiting to be 'discovered' as soon as I had drawn the first pair, which had themselves emerged naturally from the very first maps of this series, as described above.

So I added the outer spirals, doubling the height of the cone to do so, as shown in Figure 11.7, and then considered what

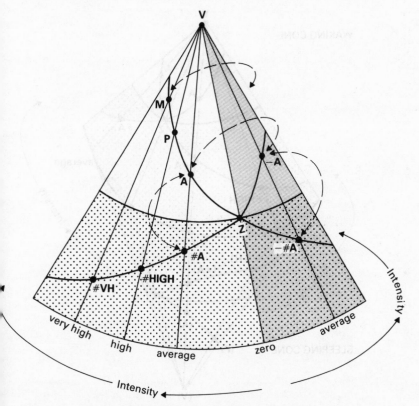

Figure 11.7 The two pairs of spirals, inner (upper) and outer (lower). Some rapid transitions added

these outer spirals might represent. I decided that they went through a region of delirium, eventually reaching one kind of coma at their common limiting point, **#MAX**. I call this point 'one type of coma', because a blow on the head, for example, might cause a different type of coma which might occur immediately without any intervening period of delirium. In such a case, starting, say, at the Average State, I would expect the representative point ψ, to drop straight down to the Origin.

Sleep was my next consideration, and I acknowledged its individual character by inverting the cone to form a spinning-top shape, as in Figure 11.8.

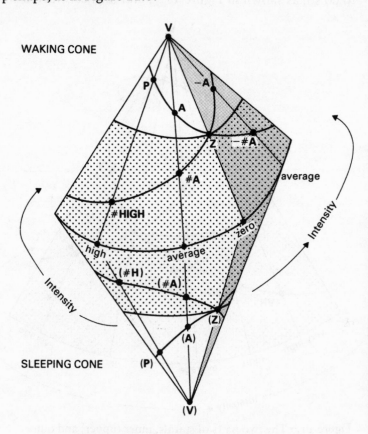

Figure 11.8 The spinning-top map

The next important modification came in about 1977 when my colleague, Dr Alan N. Fish, suggested that I needed another cone, so that one could could be 'on-line' to the outside world and the other 'off-line', as shown in Figure 11.9. About this

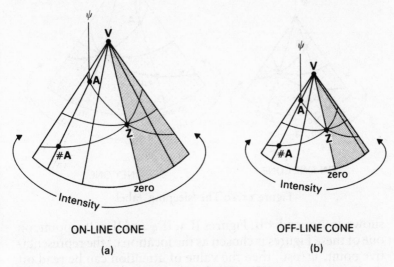

ON-LINE CONE   OFF-LINE CONE
(a)   (b)

Figure 11.9 (a) The 'on-line' cone. (b) The 'off-line' cone, shown with lower mind work

time I moved the Average State to a point halfway around the intensity dimension, as shown. This made room for a point **Ee**, to represent Eerie States. See Appendix II, Figure II.1.

Introducing the second cone led me immediately to reconsider how to portray sleep, and I stopped drawing the spinning-top map. In sleep the 'on-line' cone seems to drop down to a very small monitoring function. I still felt the need to distinguish sleep from waking states in some other way, however, and that is why I use the 'sleeping' label, as in Figure 11.10. This label emphasizes that sleep is very different from waking, even though it is hard to define in what way it is different.

Lastly, I have only recently realized that the *map* can be shown on a plane, such as a sheet of paper, without losing any information. This is because the values of things and attention can both be obtained from such two-dimensional maps, as

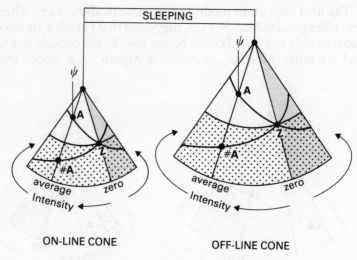

Figure 11.10 The 'sleeping' label

shown in Appendix II, Figures II.3, II.4 and II.5. If a point, on one of these Figures is chosen as the location of the representative point, ψ (psi), then the value of attention can be read off the Figure from the distance between ψ (psi), the representative point, and the circumference. The explanation of this is shown in Figure 11.11, where lines of equal length are marked. These qualities are due to the triangles involved being right-angled triangles whose other angles are both $45°$.

That ends the account of how the present *map* gradually evolved, starting with my interest in mystical language and mystical procedures. I may well have been influenced by some of the other maps, described in Chapter 10, but it is hard for me to be sure.

11.2 Chapter summary

The *map* gradually evolved, in a sequence of steps. The first step was my interest in the mystical literature which led me to make a two-dimensional map, showing intensity and things. A box-shaped map followed, adding attention. On putting the ends of the box together I formed a map like a cake with a hole

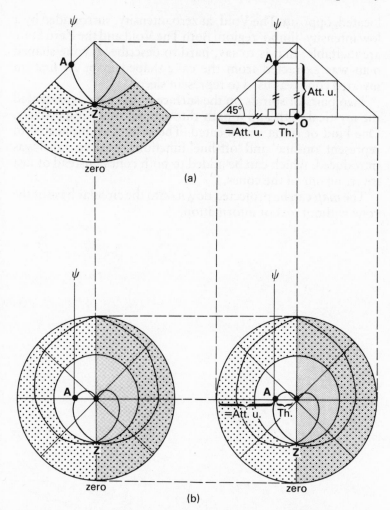

Figure 11.11 The *map* (a) as a cone, and (b) as the base of the cone

in the middle. The hole then disappeared, leaving only a vertical line.

The Mystical State Proper and the Dark Mystical State Proper were separated. The Void was then inserted between them, at the 'coincidence of contradictories'. The Average State was placed on the pleasant side. The Zero State was located, opposite The Void, at zero intensity, surrounded by a low intensity 'limbo' region. Both The Void and the Zero State are ineffable, that is to say, hard to describe. A cone-shaped map was extracted from the cake-shaped map. At first an inverted cone was used to represent sleep.

Two pairs of spirals on the surface of the cone represented the mystical path and a path through delirium, respectively. One kind of coma was located. The cone was duplicated to represent 'on-line' and 'off-line' functions. A 'sleep' label was introduced, which can be added to both cones, instead of just inverting one of the cones.

The *map* can be projected down onto the circular base of the cone without loss of information.

PART SIX

Discussion

Chapter 12 is on topics for discussion that have arisen in the course of the book.

Chapter 13 is a brief assessment of the *map*. This is an attempt by myself to point out some of the stronger and weaker points, and to come to some conclusions.

Chapter 12

Topics for discussion

In this Chapter I take several topics that have arisen, or been implied, earlier and explore them in greater depth.

12.1 Putting the network together

The network of mental states shown (in an incomplete form) in Chapter 2, Figure 2.1, was built up gradually. It was based on various pieces of information which allowed fragments of the network to be drawn. Then those fragments were put together.

To begin, there is the transition from the Average State to a Peak Experience, as described in the first chapter of D. H. Lawrence's (1921) novel *Women in Love*. These Peak Experiences gradually fade, so I show the transition as reversible:

$$A \rightleftharpoons P$$

I next assume that Mystical States Proper are the next step along this particular line:

$$A \rightleftharpoons P \rightleftharpoons M$$

Beyond that is the transition to The Void, as described in the quotation from Koestler (1954) in Section 12.5. I do not know of any descriptions of the reverse movement and so I show it by a single arrow:

$$A \rightleftharpoons P \rightleftharpoons M \rightarrow V$$

I assume that the mystics sometimes enter The Void from Dark Mystical States Proper (see Figure 12.1). This draws our attention to the parallel line of Dark States, which include the 'out-of-sorts' malaise at $-A$, and moves on to more intense states such as occur in depression (see Figure 12.2.).

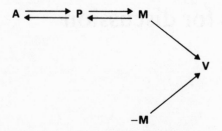

Figure 12.1 Transition to The Void from the Mystical State Proper
and from the Dark Mystical State Proper

Cross-connections now suggest themselves. These I show
with arrows made of dashed lines. I wish to indicate by these
arrows that these transitions are rapid, if not instantaneous.
This fits in with the way moods change rapidly and do not
seem to have a stable intermediate form. They are polarized
and we experience them as either pleasant or unpleasant. The
Average State, **A**, is an exception to this general rule because
we do not notice it – we are so used to its level of intensity that
we do not regard it as particularly pleasant except when we
contrast it with Dark States. See Figures 12.3 and 11.7.

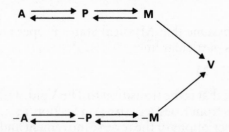

Figure 12.2 The introduction of the other Dark States

I can now add the Eerie States of depersonalization and
derealization that Sartre (1938) describes at the beginning of
his novel *Nausea* (see Chapter 6, Section 6.3) – see Figure 12.4.
I assume, by the symmetry of the network that I am building
up, that there is a dashed arrow between **Ee** and **−Ee**.

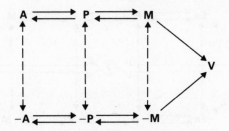

Figure 12.3 Cross-connections: rapid transitions

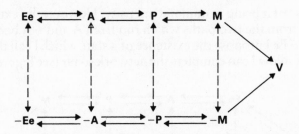

Figure 12.4 The Eerie States are added

The mystics get back from The Void to **A***, the enlightened state. I have to find this path, but I think that the section of the network in Figure 12.5 acts as a one-way 'valve'. So I must find a path that goes on, beyond **V**.

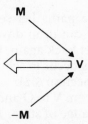

Figure 12.5 Section of the network that acts as a one-way 'valve'

Again, symmetry suggests the network in Figure 12.6, the two question marks indicating the possible position of other states. In the centre I want to put the Origin, for reasons based upon the geometry of the *map*. At the left-hand end I need a state to balance The Void, but this is a very elusive place by

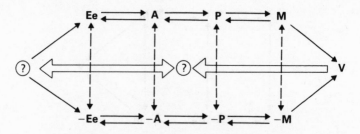

Figure 12.6 A suggested symmetrical network

virtue of it being at minimal intensity. However, by extrapola-
tion from the two paths which run from **A** and −**A** back to **Ee**
and −**Ee** I propose the existence of a state which I call the Zero
State. Now I can complete the network so far (see Figure 12.7).

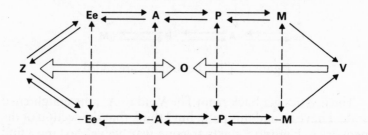

Figure 12.7 The Zero State and the Origin are added to the network

I have put reversible paths between **Z** and **Ee** and −**Ee**
because I think people can drop down into the very strange
region around **Z** and get back again. I tentatively suggest that
catatonic states, such as occur in schizophrenia, may be at or
near **Z** (see Chapter 6, Section 6.2).

The hollow arrows from **V** to **O** and **O** to **Z** indicate a rapid
if not instantaneous change of state. They represent a sudden
drop and a sudden but reversible rise in mind work respectively. In the first case the *map* collapses to a point at the Origin,
O, while in the second the *map* expands from a point at the
Origin, **O**, to become a cone again, but may collapse again as
shown by the double-ended hollow arrow from **O** to **Z**.

I think some of the mystics may stay at the Origin for some
time, and my two hollow arrows, both pointing at **O**, allow

such a stay.

The network can be extended to include diffuse states (see Figures 12.8 and 11.7). I use dashed arrows again, to indicate that these transitions, when they occur, are rapid.

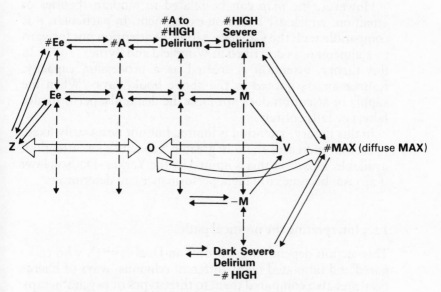

Figure 12.8 The network is extended to include diffuse states

One further extension is to indicate a transition to sleeping states by bracketing the state thus:

A ←--→(A)

However, it is not easy to add a sleeping network onto the main network, so I have not attempted to do so, although I have used the 'rapid' dashed arrow again above. This fits in with the experience of 'falling' asleep and of being woken suddenly.

All these networks can, of course, be related to the cone-shaped *map* or to the base of the cone. (More work is needed on the arrow notation to make it consistent. I do not wish to imply a path from V to O to #MAX.)

12.2. Theories of attention and the *map*

The *map* has been built up largely on the basis of the mystical literature, on descriptions of ordinary life, and on descriptions of psychiatric patients, by themselves and others.

However, the *map* can be related to modern theories of attention, which are based on experiment. In particular, it is compatible with the Capacity Model of attention put forward by Kahneman, as described in Wingfield and Byrnes (1981). In this theory, attention is treated as a processing capacity. Kahneman, as quoted in the above book, says: 'When the supply of attention does not meet the demands, performance falters or fails entirely.'

In this theory, attention is limited but not necessarily fixed. If arousal increases there is greater 'capacity', i.e. attention, available. However this is limited by the Yerkes–Dodson law: if arousal becomes too high, performance can deteriorate.

12.3 Interpreting the mystical path

This section depends a great deal on Doel (1973), who compared and tabulated many different religious 'ways of liberation' and also compared them to three types of psychotherapy – psycho-analytic, Jungian and existential. *Existentialist Theology* described by Macquarrie (1955) is also relevant to this section.

The main pattern which Doel found is that of 'spiritual death' followed by despair which leads on to a 'rebirth' of the person.

Putting these ideas into my notation, I can try to relate some of the metaphors used in these various traditions to the mental states along the mystical path.

A man puts himself into a prison of his own making, by attachment:

$$A \rightarrow |A|$$

A 'way of liberation' helps him to get out again:

$$|A| \rightarrow A^*$$

And from that enlightened state, perhaps he reverts eventually to where he began?

$$A^* \rightarrow A$$

The transition from **A** to **A***, may go through several intermediate stages and I can spread out the whole process, as in Table 12.1, showing various interpretations of each stage.

Table 12.1 raises various difficulties:

(i) It does not show Dark States, *as it should*, merely because it would then become very complicated.

(ii) It illustrates the difficulties caused by referring to more than one state by single words or phrases. For example, the word 'despair' is used here to describe $|A|$, but (apart from the fact that $-|A|$ may also be involved), the word 'despair' is often used to describe $-P$ and $-M$.

(iii) The Outsider, at $|A|$, 'sees through' attachment and is thereby separated from the majority of people, who do not. The mystic in a Dark Mystical State Proper, $-M$, feels a sense of Separation, of Disunity, $-U$. There may well be similarity between these two experiences but their levels of intensity are very different.

12.4 Conversion

Conversion, i.e. the 'passing, with a sudden upheaval, from one philosophical viewpoint to another', to give Yvonne Stevenson's (1976) definition, was discussed in detail by William James (1902). Frequently the conversion is to a religious viewpoint, but not always. It can be from Catholicism to Marxism, from Anglicanism to atheism, and so on.

John Wesley induced insecurity and anxiety in his hearers by his sermons, and then presented them with a way out of their predicament – the confession and renunciation of their sinful life up till then, and the acceptance of the Christian faith. They often felt greatly relieved, tearful and euphoric at this, and some of them experienced a violent change around of their attitude to life. Similar methods are used to this day by Christian evangelists.

Table 12.1 Interpretations of the mystical path

A ⇄	|A| ⇄	¦A¦ ⇄	P ⇄ M ⟶	V⇄O⇄Z ⇄ A*→A	
Being human	Attachment	Disillusionment	'Heaven'	Enlightenment	Being human
	'Death'	Despair		'Rebirth'	
	'Sleep'			'Awakening'	
	Error	Purgation	Illumination	Union	
	Inauthenticity	Anguish		Authenticity	
	False self			Finding the true self	
	Bondage			Liberation	
	Hubris			'Knowing thyself'	
	Separation	Being an Outsider		Belonging	
	Delusion		Bliss	Reality	

Conversions vary in their suddenness, and they may be accompanied by visual and auditory hallucinations.

By contrast with religious conversion, it is interesting to read an account of a conversion to 'humanistic atheism'. This is given in *The Hot-House Plant: an Autobiography of a Young Girl* by Yvonne Stevenson (1976), whose definition of conversion was quoted above. It is a story of liberation – liberation from a narrow, anxious and joyless kind of religion which she had absorbed in her 'rigorous, extremely class-conscious and hypocritical' household. She struggled to find her own philosophy of life and found it in one which was joyful, relaxed and enthusiastic. To her, the rejection of religion was a vital part of growing up.

The fascination of this account lies in its reversal of the usual pattern. The joy and security that many people find in religion, this author found in rejecting it. She then began to engage fully in her personal quest. For example, she would gaze for hours at her cat, trying to imitate its unhurried attitude to life, its savouring of each minute. She began to notice quite ordinary things for the first time, like the fact that trains and buses have drivers!

Her conversion experience included the hallucination of being reborn from an ape. A parallel case is the intensely emotional but, to him, religious experience which Carl G. Jung had in early adolescence, and which he describes in his autobiography *Memories, Dreams, Reflections* (1961).

On the *map* both these experiences would resemble Peak Experiences, partly Dark, and with an admixture of hallucinations. They were seen, at the time, to be profoundly significant by both authors, marking a radical change in their lives.

12.5 The varieties of ineffability

Ineffability, the inability to express something or to put something into words, was mentioned earlier, in Chapter 2 (see Section 2.1). Mystics often say that their experiences are ineffable.

However, the idea of ineffability requires further examination. First, ineffability is not always complete. There are degrees of ineffability. A person may have difficulty in describing an experience but this difficulty need not amount to a total inability to do so. Second, I think that there are four quite different types of ineffability, and perhaps even more (Clark, 1979), i.e. there are at least four different ways of not being able to say something. What is more, we can use the *map* to distinguish these four ways from each other.

The *map* thus offers a classification of ineffability.

Type I ineffability

The first type is best-known and it is the kind of ineffability most associated with the mystics. The mystical literature is full of their protestations. The mystics say that their experiences cannot be described, are beyond words, and so on. As they proceed along the mystical path towards states of higher intensity there is a tendency for these protestations to increase.

At the limit, when intensity is maximal, at The Void itself, the mystics seem to reach a truly complete ineffability. The text by al-Ghazali, quoted in Chapter 2, Section 2.2, is a brilliant attempt by a mystic to convey, in words, this absolutely unutterable experience. If, indeed, it can even be called an experience – this 'undifferentiated unity' where all distinctions have disappeared, including that between subject and object, between the knower and the known, between a person and the rest of the world.

This is the limiting case of type I ineffability. At this point nothing can be expressed because there is no-thing on the mind. All concepts have been swallowed up into complete unity – not even into one concept – because now not even one concept can be expressed, not even the idea of unity; because such a unity contains no form, no contrasts, so that nothing can be discriminated. The world is totally uniform, and this total unity defeats its own expression. It is totally ineffable.

The mystic himself has disappeared, his person absorbed into this total unity. His mental state is incapable of carrying any particular idea or image, even of himself.

However this limiting state, this extreme case of type I ineffability is preceded by increasing degrees of type I, which are, right up to the limit, only partially ineffable. The text by R. M. Bucke, again quoted in Chapter 2, Section 2.2, is still quite explicit. He mentioned only a few ideas and these are very big ones like exultation and eternal life, but he is still able to express them.

The degrees of type I ineffability are very well illustrated by the following quotation from Arthur Koestler. This describes the moments just before type I ineffability reaches its limit. It occurs in a description by Koestler (1954) of a mystical state that came upon him when he was in prison during the Spanish Civil War and liable to be taken out and shot at any time. He had been scratching some Euclid on the wall of his cell and suddenly felt himself overwhelmed by a mathematical insight of great significance. In Marghanita Laski's (1961) terminology, the mathematics, in the context of great emotional stress, had acted as a 'trigger' in starting off a mystical experience.

[His mathematical insight had swept over him 'like a wave' and he goes on to say:]

The wave had originated in an articulate verbal insight: but this evaporated at once, leaving in its wake only a wordless essence, a fragrance of eternity, a quiver of the arrow in the blue. I must have stood there for some minutes, entranced, with a wordless awareness that 'this is perfect – perfect'.

[He then recalls that he might be taken out and shot at any minute. But, at that time, this thought seemed quite trivial to him! He goes on:]

Then I was floating on my back in a river of peace, under bridges of silence. It came from nowhere and flowed nowhere. Then there was no river and no I. The I had ceased to exist.

The above passage is very intense, and it contains the ideas of:

K   Knowledge ('insight')
E   Eternity

It also, perhaps, contains:

U   Unity
J   Joy

because the last two ideas, mingled together, are implied by the words 'perfect' and 'peace'.

However, notice that Koestler goes beyond the Mystical

State Proper, **M**. He was floating 'in a river of peace' which then disappeared: 'there was no river and no I. The I had ceased to exist.' This is The Void, where Unity becomes so complete that it cannot even express the personal 'I'.

Let us now consider the ineffability of these two states, described in the quotation above. At first, in the Mystical State Proper at **M**, Koestler says that his mathematical insight became 'a wordless essence'. But, when he gets to the limit at **V**, he says nothing at all, except to say – in retrospect – that he had disappeared. 'There was no I.'

This, at last, is complete ineffability. For now there is no person to express anything. Such an absence of the person is likewise expressed by al-Ghazali, in the quotation mentioned above. In terms of the *map*, Koestler has gone from **M** to **V** along the one-way route, past a point of no return, which lies on the far side of **M**.

$$P \rightleftarrows M \rightarrow V$$

And, indeed, I do not know of any description by a mystic of his having retraced his steps from **V** to **M**, or to −**M**, directly. Once they reach **V** they seem to keep on going around the mystical path, (via **O** and **Z**?), until they return to **A***. This is why, in the network of states (Figure 2.1) I make the route through **V** a one-way route.

This one-way route acts like a valve in the mystical path, analogous to the valves in our veins which only allow the blood to flow one way, back to the heart. (One can readily demonstrate these valves in the veins in one's own forearm, as described by William Harvey (1628).)

To sum up my ideas on type I ineffability, I link it to the degree of intensity of the mental state. As intensity rises so does the degree of type I ineffability until, at the limit where intensity is maximal – at The Void – type I ineffability becomes total.

The quotation from Koestler describes this transition.

$$M \rightarrow V$$
(High intensity → Maximum intensity)
(High type I ineffability → Total type I ineffability)

Koestler, in the above quotation, describes the loss of his person that occurred with complete ineffability.

Type II ineffability
In Chapter 6, Section 6.3, I discussed the psychiatric symptoms of depersonalization and derealization. I think that these are accompanied by type II ineffability. This is the ineffability that occurs when a person moves towards the Zero State, Z, along the following route, moving from right to left along it:

$$Z \rightleftarrows Ee \rightleftarrows A$$

At one end of the *map*, near zero intensity, there is too much information for the person to make sense of the world. Everything is potentially meaningful, because everything is uncertain. The person is overwhelmed, not by increasing certainty – as in a Mystical State Proper, moving towards The Void, as described in the quotation from Koestler – but by increasing uncertainty which reaches its limit at Z.

At this limit the person disappears; not into a totally uniform state of 'undifferentiated unity', as at V, but into a completely random state at Z. This state is full of potential forms, but none are chosen with any certainty at all.

Along the route from A to Z the person finds the world, including himself, increasingly difficult to grasp. At the Eerie State, Ee, everything is eerie, with the uncanny ambiguity of a ghost story. Finally, Z is totally ambiguous, and so totally incomprehensible. Everything is there, potentially, but nothing is chosen. No particular thing has been paid for, as it were, by enough attention.

So this type of ineffability, type II, is an inability to formulate a message because the world is increasingly elusive in its uncertainty and ambiguity.

Type III ineffability
I give the name type III ineffability to a type of ineffability which is experienced by people who are enlightened, thus:

$$A \rightarrow A^*$$

Such people say that this experience, of enlightenment, is ineffable; but it may not be completely so. Descriptions of

enlightened people, by observers, often mention their unpre-
dictability. Here is a description of a Chinese sage, called here a
'man of character', by Chuang Tzu (quoted in Watts, 1957).

> The man of character lives at home without exercising his
> mind and performs actions without worry. The notions of
> right and wrong and the praise and blame of others do not
> disturb him.
>
> Sorrowful in countenance, he looks like a baby who has
> lost his mother; appearing stupid he goes about like one
> who has lost his way. He has plenty of money to spend, but
> does not know where it comes from. He drinks and eats
> just enough and does not know where it comes from.

Type IV ineffability

Finally, for my last type of ineffability, type IV, I come to the
Average State itself, at **A**. Here we have an entirely different
kind of ineffability, the ineffability of the commonplace, the
accepted, the familiar. The problem lies in the fact that we do
not always notice the ordinary until it is pointed out to us, for
example by artists, but then it may no longer seem ordinary.
For example, ordinary objects from daily life can become,
when 'found' by an artist such as Picasso, disturbing works of
art, e.g. the bull he made from a bicycle seat and a pair of
handle-bars.

It is very hard to describe the A-state. This may be because,
in its most typical, its most balanced form – the Golden
A-state – it is unself-conscious. We cannot catch it 'upon the
wing'.

This may be the greatest insight of Zen Buddhism. It elevates
ordinary life, by indicating that it is enough in itself. So why
not just 'walk on'? And 'sit when sitting', 'eat when eating',
and so on? In other words, ordinary life can be non-attached
and, when it is, how can it be distinguished from enlightenment? (See Reps, 1957; Herrigel, 1953; and Blythe, 1942.)

After all, if you are already at **A**, which may itself be the true
goal of the mystical path, then the shortest way round the
mystical path is to stay exactly where you are:

$$\overset{A}{\curvearrowleft}$$

Or just:

A

the pathless path.

The four types of ineffability

To sum up, I have related ineffability to intensity. Four varieties, or types, have been distinguished.

Type I occurs in the high intensity of Mystical States Proper, at M, (and at $-M$), and reaches its limit at The Void, at V where meaning becomes maximal but refers to nothing at all, and the person disappears.

Type II occurs in low intensity states, such as the Eerie States at Ee (and $-Ee$), and reaches its limit at the Zero State, at Z, where meaning becomes minimal but refers, potentially, to everything. Here again, in another kind of incomprehensible world, the person disappears.

Type III and type IV both occur at average levels of intensity, but are just as baffling as types I and II, which occur at more exotic places. Type III occurs in the elusive state of 'enlightenment', at A^*, while type IV occurs in ordinary life, in the Average State of mind at A. We simply do not notice type IV by virtue of its extreme familiarity and hence cannot describe it. This is the Golden A-state.

(Sleep, at (A), and relaxation as in a daydream, at $\#A$, are also essential but it is the fully awake A-state at A, alert and balanced, which I wish to call the Golden A-state.)

The above four types of ineffability are displayed, related to their corresponding degrees of intensity, in Figure 12.9.

Another way of classifying ineffability

Here is another way of classifying ineffability, suggested by my colleague, Dr Alan N. Fish.

If we consider a communication channel, thus:

message

Sender ⟶ Receiver

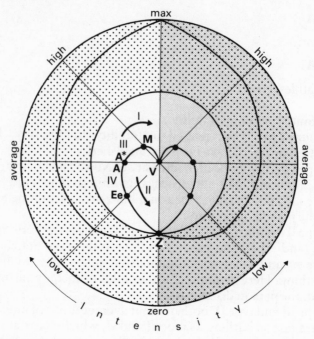

Figure 12.9 Four types of ineffability (shown on one side of the
map only), related to intensity

then we can relate the four kinds of ineffability to it.

In type I there is a message; it is one of extreme Unity, and so
on. It is hard to formulate because of its unusual intensity.
Moreover, as the person approaches **V** he himself loses the
qualities of a person, being swallowed up by the prevailing
Unity, so that he can no longer act as Sender.

In type II there is a message that is very hard to formulate
because of its increasing ambiguity. At the limit, the message
becomes totally random and the person cannot even compre-
hend himself as a person and can no longer act as a Sender,
even of a random message.

In type III the Sender can appear to be very normal and
lucid and yet the message itself is peculiarly baffling. At one
level it can be understood, in that it can be couched in ordinary
language. However, the Receiver, though trying hard to
understand the nature of enlightenment, may fail to under-

stand the message. Zen Buddhist literature is full of messages of this enigmatic cast. The dawning ability to understand these enigmas is used as a measure of progress towards enlightenment.

In type IV there is an even stranger barrier to communication. The Average State, A, is unself-conscious – at least, it is when in its most gloriously unobtrusive form, the Golden A-state. It follows, therefore, that a person cannot describe this state, because to do so he must be self-conscious and when he is self-conscious he can no longer be in this state. So, if he does describe this state, he doesn't! And vice versa.

In other words, in type IV the act of description changes what is being described. The message itself changes what it is about, the mental state of the Sender. The message, which purports to describe the Sender, changes the Sender and so, when sent, is incorrect.

Figure 12.10 relates the four types of ineffability to the communication channel, indicating which parts of the channel are affected in each type, while Table 12.2 gives a summarized explanation.

Table 12.2 A summarized explanation of the types of ineffability

Ineffability	Explanation
Type I	As intensity increases, words are less adequate to express the concepts of the Sender and more incomprehensible to the Receiver. At the limit no words are suitable at all.
Type II	As intensity decreases, the Sender's concepts become more and more meaningless in themselves, even before their expression is attempted.
Type III	An enlightened person can express himself quite 'clearly' and may consider that he has produced an adequate message, but the concepts understood by the Receiver may be meaningless.
Type IV	There can be no correct message. ('In everyday life, one does not describe it!') Therefore the presence of a message changes the state it purports to describe and hence renders the message incorrect.

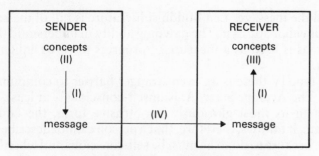

Figure 12.10 The four types of ineffability related to a communication channel

12.6 'A temporary crystallization of the mind'

T. S. Eliot (1931) used the phrase, 'a temporary crystallization of the mind' when talking about mystical experience. Following this hint, I have speculated along the following lines.

Suppose that the subjective sense of certainty that accompanies the intensity variable is related to the self-agreement of the attention units. I mean by self-agreement that they resemble each other. If they were simple 'on–off' switches, for example, then total self-agreement would be for them to be all 'on' or all 'off'. If this self-agreement can vary, then one could imagine counting how many switches were 'on' and how many 'off'. Then a percentage could be worked out of the predominant switches – 70 per cent 'on', say, or 80 per cent 'off'.

Next, I consider what conditions might help the self-agreement percentage to rise. First of all, an increase in the concentration ratio would reduce the things to which attention was to be paid and would increase the surplus of attention units. If the ratio becomes very high, as in some kinds of meditation, then things practically disappear, leaving a great deal of surplus attention. However, meditation does not lead to a rise in intensity all at once. Practice seems to be required. Perhaps also the orientation procedures adopted by meditators – 'preliminary Yoga', the thinking and acting along the prescribed lines of the particular tradition – perhaps all these are catalysts?

If the 'spare' attention units do suddenly agree with each other, like a crystal which forms itself suddenly in a supersaturated solution, then could not that account for the sudden onset so characteristic of mystical states?

Other causes of self-agreement need to be found for mental illnesses. (Slater and Roth (1977), have surveyed the research which has long sought for some psychedelic substance formed in the body in mental illness, and analogous to the psychedelic drugs in its effects.)

This Section, Section 12.6, has been an attempt to tackle the problem of mysticism which was stated in Chapter 2, Section 2.8.

12.7 Chapter summary

Several topics are discussed in greater depth than earlier in the book.

I first describe how I pieced the network of states together, using symmetry as a guide, and hoping it has not misled me.

Then, I briefly refer to Kahneman's Capacity Model of attention which is, at least, compatible with the *map*.

Next I tabulate various interpretations of the mystical path. This is followed by a brief discussion of conversion and a comparison of two autobiographies.

The varieties of ineffability are then analysed at some length. Four different ways of not being able to say something are described. These four types are related to intensity. They are also analysed in terms of a communication channel.

Lastly, I speculate upon T. S. Eliot's description of mystical experience as 'a temporary crystallization of the mind'. I put forward the idea of the 'self-agreement' of attention units in an attempt to account for the sense of subjective certainty described by the mystics and others.

Chapter 13

Brief assessment of the *map*

As I have developed the *map* I have been intermittently aware of both its stronger, and its weaker points. In emulation of Charles Darwin I have noted them down at once, especially the weaker ones.

So, in this chapter I consider the stronger points first, as objectively as I can, then restore the balance by stating what I think are the weaker points. Lastly, I try to sum up the pros and cons in a brief assessment of the *map* which should at least help my critics to focus their attacks.

13.1 Stronger points

The *map* is conceptually simple and easy to use

The map *has a simple geometric shape*
This simplicity is an advantage because the properties of the *map* can easily be grasped by non-mathematicians.

The use of ordinary language and standard psychiatric terminology
Apart from the term 'mind work', I have not coined any new words or phrases. My use of plain English and standard psychiatric terminology (as used in Slater and Roth, 1977) should be a source of strength to the *map*.

The map *can be put onto computer graphics*
Computer graphics, produced by programs such as that contained in Appendix I, and more advanced versions of it, could

provide pictures of the *map* which would show the characteristic sequences of mental states in various conditions.

The map *feels 'natural'*
The *map* provides a descriptive framework for mental states which feels 'natural' to use. I have often found that a person, on being shown it, starts to use it at once, together with its terminology.

The map *is convenient to use*
Related to the above claim, that the *map* feels natural, is the claim that it is convenient to use. In particular I think that mental states can be shown on the *map* quickly and clearly. Extra variables can be added, as required, to the main variables. Then, with a little practice the whole mental state can be taken in at a glance.

The map *might be useful in teaching, especially in psychiatry*
Should the *map* prove acceptable as an educational method, in say psychiatry, then it could provide a new way of displaying the above sequences. Existing descriptions of mental illnesses, as found in textbooks, are usually very condensed. They are highly edited summaries of sequences of the mental states of one or more patients.

This lack of adequate detail of sequences of mental states is probably due, partly, to the lack of a convenient method for displaying them. The *map*, especially when displayed on computer graphics, might encourage a more systematic collection of these elusive and fluctuating details.

Ordinary life, and the neuroses, and the psychoses, all differ in terms of the changes in the main variables of the *map*, especially when the timing and duration of these changes are also taken into account. The use of computer graphics, in association with the *map*, might help to emphasize these characteristic differences.

The *map* displays existing knowledge well

The map *attempts to be comprehensive*
Maybe any map of the mind that is comprehensive enough to

encompass some aspects of ordinary life, mental illnesses, drug states and mysticism represents a step forward!

Chapter 10 was a survey of other psychological maps. The question arises whether my *map* is a true advance on the others or whether its disadvantages, some of which I will list shortly in Section 13.2, outweigh the good points.

The mystical path is represented on the map *as a path that returns to its beginnings*
This is an important point, because this is how the mystical path is often described. What is more it gives the *map* one of its most important features, the semi-circular intensity dimension. The point about this circularity is that mental variables reach limits when a person goes a long way in any direction. At such limits dramatic changes occur, such as the entry into The Void from the Mystical State Proper.

Subtle changes, from state to state, can be easily detected on the map
When following the course of a person through a sequence of mental states on the *map*, the eye can easily detect small changes. This is one of the main advantages of using a geometrical representation of mental states.

Overlapping features of the different kinds of mental life can be studied
The four different kinds of mental life – ordinary, abnormal, artificial and unusual – are neither identical nor entirely different. There are important overlapping features and these can be shown. The temporal sequences of mental states are important when making these discriminations.

The map *enables characteristic sequences of mental states to be recognized*
This is related to the last point. Moreover, this feature of the *map* should be greatly improved by using computer graphics.

The *map* suggests new interpretations

The map *makes important distinctions*
The *map* separates variables which otherwise tend to be bundled together, or even confused, in descriptions of mental states. Mind work, i.e. excitement or lethargy, type of mood, intensity of mood, confusion, distortion of perception and thinking, anxiety and poor concentration, can all be displayed on the *map* separately. This separation is important, particularly in psychiatry.

For example, a schizophrenic can have a clear, that is to say an unconfused, mind, but, nevertheless, a mind containing distortions of perception and of thinking, i.e. hallucinations and delusions. Such a person may also, at the same time, be anxious or not, and may also be excited, or have average mind work, or be lethargic.

To take another example, consider a healthy person having a daydream of the confused, vague, 'dreamy' sort – the kind that is hard to remember. Such a person is neither hallucinated nor deluded and is unlikely to be anxious or excited, but may be lethargic.

By contrast with both the schizophrenic and the healthy daydreamer described above, consider a person suffering from a delirium, say delirium tremens. Such a person may vary in general mood from pleasant to unpleasant. He is also likely to be confused and anxious, and to be suffering from delusions and hallucinations – typically of small animals.

The three people described above are experiencing very different mental states and, what is more, very different sequences of mental states in time. Mere verbal descriptions do not bring out these important differences in the way that the *map* does.

The map *suggests new approaches to problems*
For example, the *map* has made me try to classify daydreams (see Chapter 1, Section 1.1), and to think about the ways patients go in and out of coma. Coma is not always preceded by delirium, as the path down the outer spiral to #**MAX** might imply (see Chapter 6, Section 6.2).

Catatonic states are described in terms of the map
Descriptions of severe catatonic states are usually rather baffling. I hope that locating them at the Zero State, Z, on the *map* will suggest new insights into their nature. The fact that Z can be excited or lethargic is important, because catatonic excitement and stupor can both occur.

'Models' of manic-depressive illness can be related to the map
It may be possible to resolve the difference between models which show the illness like this:

Normality $\rightleftarrows$ Depression $\rightleftarrows$ Mania

and those which show it like this:

Mania $\rightleftarrows$ Normality $\rightleftarrows$ Depression

The *map* is open to validation

As a method of clinical description
The cone itself, before the spirals are added and before particular points are identified with particular mental states, is a method of clinical description, and nothing more. It only assumes that the dimensions exist and are measurable.

To show that the dimensions of the *map* are relevant in the description of mental states, observers should be asked to classify patients' mental states according to existing conventions, and also to rate them on each of the three dimensions – things, attention and intensity – or the equivalent three dimensions – concentration ratio, mind work and intensity. A point representing each observation should then be plotted on the *map*. If all the points representing a particular mental state (as classified by convention, e.g. a manic state) cluster in one portion of the *map*, and if all such clusters are separate and distinct on the *map*, then the map would have been validated as a method of clinical description.

As a scientific theory
The cone with the spirals added and with particular points identified with particular mental states constitutes a scientific theory. The above two sets of 'markings' represent hypotheses,

e.g. the hypothesis that 'normal' mental states tend to occur along the spirals, or that this or that particular combination of values of the three dimensions occurs in particular, named, mental states.

Any clusters that are found in the description of mental states should now be compared with the spirals and the identified mental states on the *map*. Any agreement between the clusters and these 'markings' would support the hypotheses that the markings represent. Any disagreements would cast doubt upon those hypotheses and suggest new ones.

The validation described above for the use of the *map* as a method of clinical description is a necessary condition of the validation described here, of the *map* as a scientific theory.

(The discussion, above, of the two kinds of validation, I owe to Dr Alan N. Fish.)

13.2 Weaker points

The map varies in its ability to display various mental states

The portrayal of sleep and dreams is inadequate
The indication of the difference between being asleep and awake, merely by the use of a special 'marker', reveals a topic on the *map* which needs much development.

Hallucinations and delusions need extra variables
The occurrence of hallucinations and delusions can only be indicated on the *map* by the use of extra variables. This is unsatisfactory, since they are important psychiatric symptoms. Moreover, the specific type of hallucination, or delusion, in different psychoses must also be specified.

Schizophrenia is difficult to plot on the map
This difficulty relates directly to that of dealing with hallucinations and delusions, since they are both very important symptoms in schizophrenia. (However, see the paragraph on catatonic states in Section 13.1 above and also note that the region around Z, where intensity is low, provides a place where the perplexity and also, perhaps, the apathy of some schizophrenic states may belong.)

Theoretical weaknesses

The Origin and the Zero State
There is a weakness in the argument about the Origin and the Zero State occurring on the Mystical Path. I have placed them on it for theoretical reasons, so as to complete the circle of the mystical path.

The aspects of mind going up and down together
I assume that, as intensity changes, the set of aspects of mind all go up and down together with it. I expect there are many exceptions to this and, indeed, there may be characteristic 'profiles' of the various aspects in various states of mind.

The map requires extra variables
The extra variables, which I have to tag on to the *map* at times, are a confession of failure. They are necessary because the *map* has very few main variables. However, I prefer to add them baldly rather than to try and cram them in by some new, and arbitrary, extended use of the main variables.

My analysis of mystical texts is only informal
I have not tabulated the various items and then done a formal count of them in a representative sample of texts, in the manner adopted by Laski (1961).

13.3 Conclusions

Briefly, I can sum up the stronger points by saying that the *map* feels 'natural', that it keeps some important variables clearly separated, and that it may be a convenient method of displaying sequences of mental states, especially in mental illnesses. On the other hand, some weaker points are that it needs extra variables, it does not represent sleep and dreams adequately, and that it is not easy to represent schizophrenia on it.

Time will tell whether the *map* is useful as it stands and whether it stimulates work to improve it. In particular, clinical research would be needed to validate my descriptions of mental illnesses, drug states, mystical states and ordinary life states.

The basic problem, as I see it, when mapping the mind, is how to cram enough variables onto a map without it losing the quality of being easy to take in at a glance.

More advanced mathematical methods, such as the use of matrices, might be better able to cope with the complexity of the mind than my use of a simple geometric figure. Nevertheless, they might deter many people whom I would like to interest in the *map*.

One way round this dilemma might be to have a set of complementary maps, each fairly simple and each dealing with a few variables. The use of on-line and off-line cones is, already, an example of this principle.

13.4 Chapter summary

Some of the stronger and weaker points of the *map* are listed and a brief evaluation is attempted in Section 13.3.

This also includes a brief discussion of the basic problem when mapping the mind, i.e. how to display a large number of important mental variables without overcrowding the map.

The use of various sets of complementary maps is a possible solution, as already exemplified in the use of separate *maps* for on-line and off-line functions.

General summary

This book presents a *map* of mental states, a map of the mind. This is based largely on the literature of mysticism, which describes an unusual but recognizable path, the Mystical Path, as it passes through a characteristic series of mental states. This path is well-known and is treasured in many ancient traditions throughout the world. The other important source of the *map* is our daily experience of ordinary life, together with the literature which describes it.

However, the *map* enables a wider range of mental states to be plotted than just those of mysticism and ordinary life. States encountered in mental illnesses and after taking certain drugs, including the psychedelic drugs such as cannabis and LSD, can also be plotted.

The *map* has the shape of a cone. The radius, height and angular dimension of the cone represent the mental variables of things, attention and the intensity of general mood, respectively. The surface of the cone is sub-divided twice. First, so as to represent pleasant and unpleasant general moods. Second, to represent zones of concentrated and diffuse thinking. The cone also varies in height: a larger cone represents a more excited state than a smaller one.

The *map*, as the curved surface of a cone, can also be projected down onto its circular base, without loss of information.

On-line functions and off-line functions are represented simultaneously by using two separate cones, one for each function.

Sleep is indicated by a special marker and by an emphasis on the off-line cone. This is where dreams are shown occurring, especially when rapid eye movements (REM) occur during 'paradoxical' sleep.

The main variables of the *map* – things and attention units – generate two functions, their ratio and their sum, which are called concentration ratio and mind work respectively. The latter is equivalent to 'general arousal'. Both the concentration ratio and mind work are represented on the cone.

'Extra' variables are added, in the captions, to indicate the presence of symptoms such as anxiety, compulsions or phobias.

The *map* allows the mental state of a person to be plotted at a series of particular moments. A sequence of representative points thus indicates the person's journey in time through his own mental states.

The *map* tries to be comprehensive, in the sense that not only ordinary but also unusual, abnormal and artificial mental states can all be plotted on it – the ordinary states of everyday life, the unusual states of mysticism, the abnormal states of mental illnesses, and the artificial states induced by drugs. By plotting the characteristic patterns of journeys, undertaken in all four kinds of mental life, the similarities and dissimilarities between these journeys emerge and can be discussed.

Computer graphics provide a convenient medium for studying these characteristic sequences of mental states. An Appendix (Appendix I) contains a computer graphics program which draws the *map*.

An attempt is also made to relate states of mind on the *map* to mythology and the arts.

In conclusion, the main aim has been to collect together a wide selection of statements about the human mind, from fields which are not often seen to be related – ordinary life, mysticism, mental illnesses and drug states. I have tried to provide an overall descriptive framework for all the above in the form of a *map* of mental states.

The novelty of the present book lies, not in its data, which are, in the main, already available, but in the way it points to some of the common features underlying these data and draws a *map* to display them.

Finally, I hope that this *map* will be useful, particularly to psychologists and physicians, and that it will also be of general interest.

Appendices

Appendices

Appendix I

Computer graphics program

(by Dr Alan N. Fish)

This program is designed for use with an Apple II microcomputer having a visual display unit and two manual devices, called 'paddles', for controlling two variables. The program is written in APPLESOFT, a form of BASIC.

The two paddles enable the cone to be viewed from different angles and from different heights. The program draws the cone of the *map* in different sizes. The program draws lines, representing different intensities, and the two spiral lines. It also draws a very small circle or 'blob' to mark the position of the representative point.

The reason for including this program is to encourage readers to write more advanced programs, some perhaps for more elaborate computer graphics facilities. Such programs could, for example, vary the size of the cone continuously and thus show different mind work levels without having to redraw the whole *map*. They could also duplicate the cone for on-line and off-line functions, and label the various dimensions.

Most important of all, they could show the representative point moving from one place to another. This would allow the journeys described in this book to be seen in progress. The time variable could be speeded up so that hours, days or weeks would appear to pass in a matter of seconds. This would enable the viewer to recognize the characteristic patterns, in time, of various journeys through ordinary life, mental illnesses, drug states and mystical states. Computer tapes could then be exchanged by those interested, so that anyone with the appropriate computer graphics terminal could display the same patterns. Such patterns could also be recorded on video-tape. In the following program do not confuse the numeral 1 with the letter I.

The program (written in APPLESOFT)

```
 2  Q0 = - 16287:Q1 = - 16286:PL = 147

10  PI = 3.14159265
20  CX = 140:CY = 80
30  REM "REM" MEANS A REMARK, A COMMENT
40  TEXT
45  REM INSTRUCTIONS
50  HOME : PRINT "JOHN H. CLARK'S MAP OF
    MENTAL STATES": PRINT " =========
    ============================ "
51  PRINT "(1983 VERSION)"
52  REM THERE ARE 36 DASHES IN LINE 50
55  PRINT : PRINT "INSTRUCTIONS:": PRINT
60  PRINT "THE MAP IS IN THE SHAPE OF A CONE.":
    PRINT
65  PRINT "THE    VERTICAL    DIMENSION    IS
    'ATTENTION',"
66  PRINT "THE RADIAL DIMENSION IS 'THINGS',"
67  PRINT "THE    ANGULAR    DIMENSION    IS
    'INTENSITY'.": PRINT
70  PRINT "YOU ENTER THE COORDINATES OF A
    POINT"
71  PRINT "ON THE SURFACE OF THE CONE,"
72  PRINT "AND SET THE ROTATION AND TILT OF
    THE"
73  PRINT "CONE BY TURNING THE PADDLES
    ('PDL')."
75  PRINT
80  PRINT "THE OVERALL SIZE OF THE CONE IS
    GIVEN"
81  PRINT "BY ATT+TH. THIS MUST NOT EXCEED
    1.0."
85  PRINT "E.G. FOR THE MAXIMUM SIZE OF CONE"
86  PRINT "AT THE 'A-STATE':"
```

```
 87 PRINT "ATT=.75; TH=.25; INT=.5."
 98 PRINT : INPUT "PRESS RETURN TO
    CONTINUE"; A$
100 HGR: PRINT: PRINT: PRINT
105 REM READ A,T,I
110 INPUT "ATTENTION (FROM 0 TO 1)?";A
120 INPUT "THINGS (FROM 0 TO 1)?";T
130 INPUT "INTENSITY (FROM −1 TO 1)?";I1
135 REM MINDWORK
140 MW = A + T
141 IF MW < = 1 GOTO 150
142 PRINT "ATT+TH MUST NOT EXCEED 1.0!"
143 GOTO 110
145 REM HORIZ. AND VERT. SCALES OF CONE
150 SX = 75 * MW:SY = − 75 * MW
155 REM READ ORIENTATION OF CONE
160 HCOLOR = 3
200 PRINT "<MAX...........ZERO><
    SIDE..........PLAN>          TO   ROTATE   CONE
                  TO TILT CONE              TURN PDL
    0              TURN PDL 1        THEN PRESS
    PDL BUTTON 0 (1 TO RESTART)";
205 REM THERE ARE 11 AND 10 FULL STOPS, THEN 3,
    7, 9, 10 AND 5 SPACES, IN LINE 200
500 IF PEEK (Q0)> PL THEN 600
510 IF PEEK (Q1)> PL THEN 100
520 FOR P = 0 TO 1
530 AD(P) = 14800 + INT ( PDL (P)/12.8) + P * 20
540 POKE LAD(P),0: POKE AD(P), 127
550 LAD(P) = AD(P)
560 NEXT P: GOTO 500
600 P0 = 255 − PDL (0):P1 = PDL (1)
605 REM HORIZONTAL VIEWING ANGLE
610 VH = P0 * PI/255 − PI/2
615 REM VERTICAL VIEWING ANGLE
620 VV = P1 * PI/510
625 REM SEE NOTE 1 BELOW
630 R = SIN (VV)
635 H = SIN (PI / 2 − VV)
636 IF R < H THEN 641
```

```
640  AV = − 1: GOTO 645
641  X = R / H
642  AV = − ATN (X / SQR ( − X ∗ X + 1)) + 1.5708
645  HGR
647  REM SEE NOTE 2 BELOW
648  REM DRAW ELLIPSE AT BASE
650  A = 0:GOSUB 1000
651  REM DRAW ELLIPSE HALFWAY UP
655  A = .5:GOSUB 1000
656  REM DRAW SIDES
660  GOSUB 5000
665  REM DRAW "LONGITUDES"
680  GOSUB 3000
685  REM DRAW SPIRALS
690  GOSUB 4000
695  REM DRAW BLOB AT A,T,I
700  GOSUB 6000
900  GOTO 500
1000 REM DRAW ELLIPSE AT HEIGHT A
1010 P = 0
1020 FOR TH = 0 TO PI ∗ 2 + .1 STEP .1
1025 IF ABS (TH − PI /2)> AV THEN 1030
1026 P = 0: GOTO 1060
1030 X = COS (TH) ∗ SX ∗ (1 − A) + CX
1040 Y = R ∗ SIN(TH) ∗ SY ∗ (1 − A) + CY + A∗ H ∗ SY
1045 IF P = 1 THEN 1050
1046 HPLOT X,Y
1047 P = 1: GOTO 1060
1050 HPLOT TO X,Y
1060 NEXT TH
1100 RETURN
2000 REM DRAW "POLE"
2010 HPLOT CX,CY
2020 HPLOT TO CX,H ∗ SY + CY
2030 RETURN
2500 REM DRAW "GREENWICH MERIDIAN"
2505 IF ABS (VH − PI / 2)< = AV THEN RETURN
2510 HPLOT COS (VH) ∗ SX + CX,R ∗ SIN (VH) ∗ SY + CY
2520 HPLOT TO CX,H ∗ SY + CY
```

```
2530  RETURN
3000  REM DRAW "LONGITUDES"
3010  FOR I = - .75 TO 1 STEP .25
3020  TH = - 1 * I * PI + VH
3025  IF TH<0 THEN TH = TH + 2 * PI
3026  IF ABS (TH - PI / 2)< = AV THEN 3050
3030  HPLOT COS (TH) * SX + CX,R * SIN (TH) * SY + CY
3040  HPLOT TO CX,H * SY + CY
3050  NEXT I
3060  RETURN
4000  REM DRAW SPIRALS
4010  FOR S = - 1 TO 1 STEP 2
4015  P = 0
4020  FOR I = - 1 TO 1 STEP .02
4030  A = (1 + S * I) / 2
4040  TH = - 1 * I * PI + VH
4045  IF TH<0 THEN TH = TH + 2 * PI
4046  IF ABS (TH - PI / 2)> AV THEN 4050
4047  P = 0: GOTO 4080
4050  X = COS (TH) * SX * (1 - A) + CX
4060  Y = R * SIN (TH) * SY * (1 - A) + CY + A * H * SY
4065  IF P = 1 THEN 4070
4066  HPLOT X,Y
4067  P = 1: GOTO 4080
4070  HPLOT TO X,Y
4080  NEXT I
4090  NEXT S
4100  RETURN
5000  REM DRAW SIDES
5005  IF H < = R THEN RETURN
5010  FOR S = - 1 TO 1 STEP 2
5020  TH = PI / 2 + S * AV
5030  HPLOT COS (TH) * SX + CX,R * SIN(TH) * SY + CY
5040  HPLOT TO CX,CY + H * SY
5050  NEXT S
5060  RETURN
6000  REM DRAW BLOB
6001  IF MW = 0 THEN X1 = CX: Y1 = CY: GOTO 6060
6010  TH = - 1 * I1 * PI + VH
6020  IF TH < 0 THEN TH = TH + 2 * PI
```

```
6030  IF ABS (TH − PI / 2)< = AV THEN RETURN
6040  X1 = COS (TH) * SX * T / MW + CX
6050  Y1 = R * SIN (TH) * SY * T / MW + CY + (MW − T) *
      H * SY / MW
6055  HPLOT X1 + 4,Y1
6060  FOR SH = 0 TO 2.2 * PI STEP PI / 4
6070  HPLOT TO COS (SH) * 4 + X1, SIN (SH) * 4 + Y1
6080  NEXT SH
6090  RETURN
```

Notes on the above computer graphics program

(1)
Figures I.1, I.2 and I.3 relate to lines 630 to 642 above. VH is
the horizontal viewing angle, VV is the vertical viewing angle.

The cone shown in Figure I.2 can be imagined to be a
compressed form of Figure I.3 – a circle and two tangents. This
provides a means of calculating the apparent position of the
sides of the cone.

(2)
This note relates to lines 648 to 700 above.

These are an arbitrary selection of the graphical subroutines
(1000, 2000, 2500, 3000, 4000, 5000 and 6000). By changing
line 680 to GOSUB 2000, for instance, a cone could be drawn
with no surface lines, but with the vertical axis instead. Adding
670 GOSUB 2500 would replace one surface line – the one
which passes through the Z-state. Any combination of
GOSUBs may be used in lines 660 to 890 to produce the
desired picture.

(3)
Some interesting values, for attention, things and intensity,
are: .25, .75, .5; .5, .5, 0; .25, .25, 0; 1, 0, 1; 0, 1, 1; .75, .25,
− .5; and 0, 0, 0 (wait!).

Printout of the computer graphics program

The following printouts show the Average State marked, by
the blob, on the *map*. The *map* is seen from a range of different
heights in Figures I.4–I.8.

There is also a range of different horizontal viewing angles, from Figures I.9–I.12. Two Figures, Figures I.5 and I.11, are the same.

The Figures I.4–I.11 can be arranged in the form of a cross, as shown in Figure I.13.

The scales below each of Figures I.4–I.12 indicate the settings of the paddles. They could be labelled as shown in Figure I.14.

Figure I.8 corresponds to the *map* projected down onto the base of the cone.

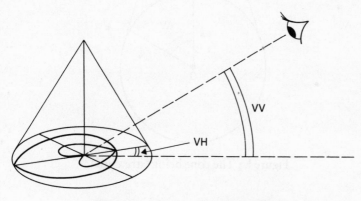

Figure I.1 The two viewing angles

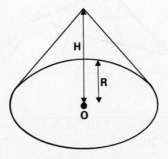

Figure I.2 The apparent height and apparent radius of the tilted cone

There it also occurs in the full frontal view, as seen from figures I.2 and I.3 below. Figures I.2 and I.3 are therefore [...]

The figure I.3 [...] can be compared to the form of a cross [...] as seen in figure I.2.

[...] below, valid for the real [...] in addition, the [...] of the public. [...] would be adapted as shown in figure I.4.

Figure I.4 corresponds to the cone passed down onto the base of the cone.

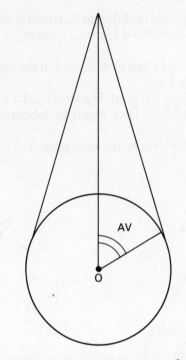

Figure I.3 The cone being 'stretched'

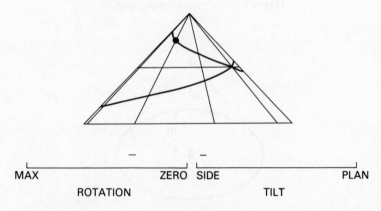

MAX		ZERO	SIDE		PLAN
	ROTATION			TILT	

Figure I.4 The cone seen from different heights: side view, 0°

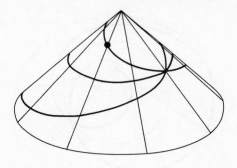

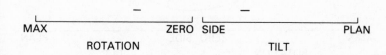

Figure I.5 The cone seen from different heights: 22.5°

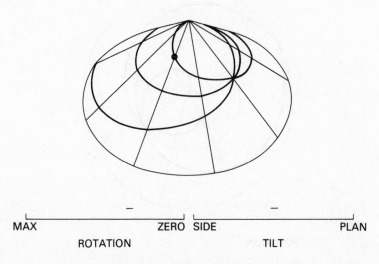

Figure I.6 The cone seen from different heights: 45°

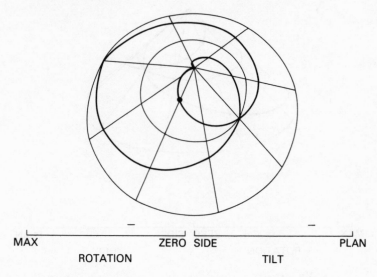

Figure I.7 The cone seen from different heights: 67.5°

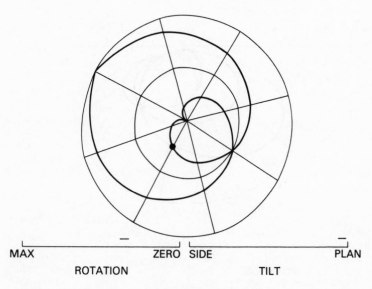

Figure I.8 The cone seen from different heights: plan view, 90°

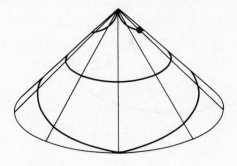

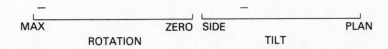

Figure I.9 The cone seen from different horizontal angles: facing maximum intensity

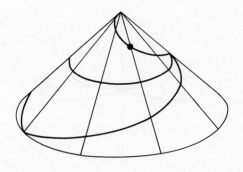

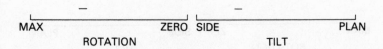

Figure I.10 The cone seen from different horizontal angles: facing average to high intensity

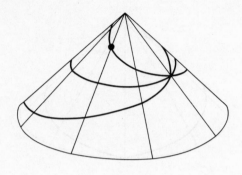

Figure I.11 The cone seen from different horizontal angles: facing average to low intensity

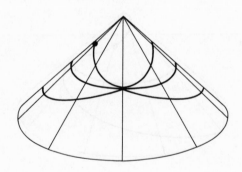

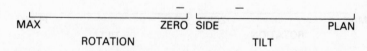

Figure I.12 The cone seen from different horizontal angles: facing zero intensity

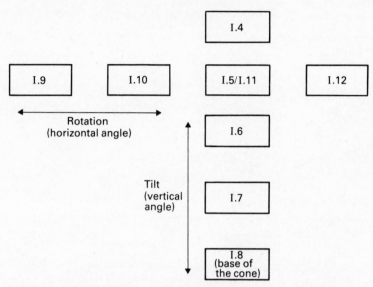

Figure I.13 Figures I.4–I.12 arranged to show their range of rotation and tilt (the two variables controlled by the paddles)

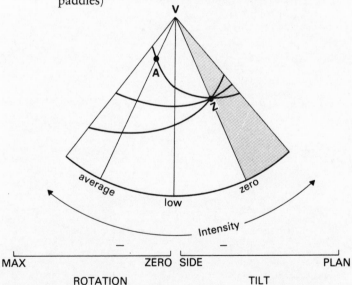

Figure I.14 The scales, as used in Figures I.4–I.12. This Figure corresponds to Figure I.5/I.11. The dashes above the scales indicate the settings of the paddles

Appendix II

Paper models of the *map* as a cone or the base of the cone

A set of *maps*, with several different levels of mind work, can readily be made. With them the reader can follow the sequences of mental states in the present book and explore other sequences.

The *map*, in its form as a cone, can be constructed by drawing the shapes shown in Figures II.1 and II.2 on thick paper. The spirals cross the straight lines at points which are 1/8 of *L*, 1/4 of *L* and so on.

If three different values of *L* are used, then cones for high, average and low mind work can be constructed. Other cones could be made to show intermediate values, for example between average and high mind work. The shorter length, *l*, can be varied for convenience, but it should be big enough to allow for the lettering.

The two sides of the cone are glued together by using the tabs labelled 'glue here'.

Copies of the *map*, in its form as the base of the cone, can be traced from Figures II.3, II.4 and II.5.

A small ψ can be made as shown in Figure II.6. It can either be stuck directly into the *map*, or into a small blob of Plasticine or Blu-Tack which is stuck onto the surface of the *map*.

Other models could be made of the *map*, to show the on-line and off-line cones simultaneously. A 'sleeping' label could also be used.

Sequences of mental states could be photographed to make sets of slides which could be shown in sequence.

(N.B. *The following cut-out Figures could be photocopied or xeroxed, to avoid damaging the book.*)

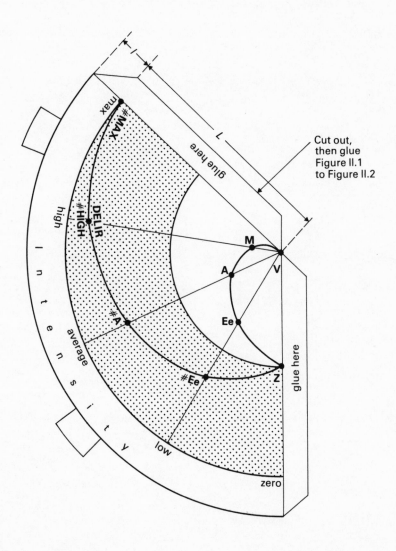

Figure II.1 The cone, pleasant side

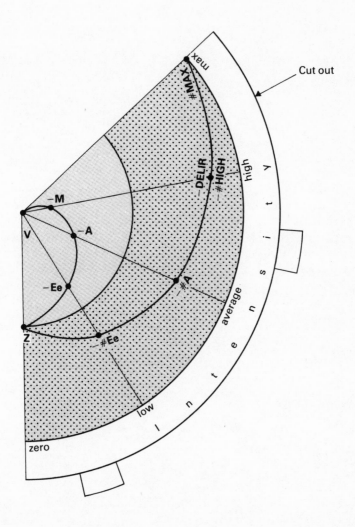

Figure II.2 The cone, unpleasant side

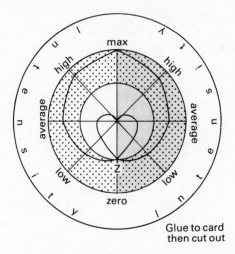

Figure II.3 The base of the cone: mind work – low

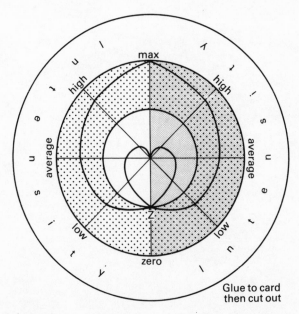

Figure II.4 The base of the cone: mind work – average

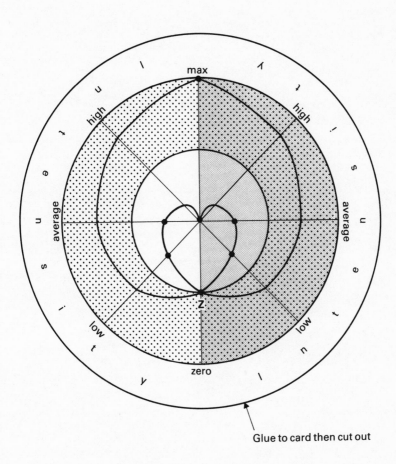

Figure II.5 The base of the cone: mind work – high

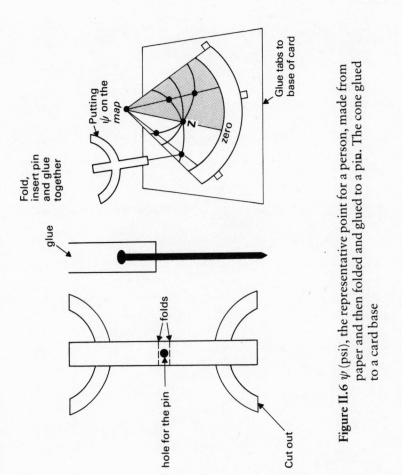

Figure II.6 ψ (psi), the representative point for a person, made from paper and then folded and glued to a pin. The cone glued to a card base

References

Aickman, R. (1964), *Dark Entries*, Fontana, London.
Ambler, E. (1940), *Journey into Fear*, Fontana, London, 1973.
Apuleius, L. (1950), *The Golden Ass*, translated by Graves, R.,
 Penguin Books, Harmondsworth.
Ashby, W. R. (1960), *Design for a Brain*, 2nd ed. revised, Chapman
 & Hall, London.
Berlyne, D. E. (1969), 'The development of the concept of attention
 in psychology', in Evans, C. R. and Mulholland, T. B. (eds),
 Attention in Neurophysiology, Butterworth, London.
Bhagavad-Gita. See Prabhavananda and Isherwood (1947).
Blake, W. (c.1808), *Milton* (edited and with a commentary by
 Easson, K. P. and Easson, R. R.), Shambhala Publications,
 Boulder, Colorado, in association with Random House, New
 York, 1978.
Blakemore, C. B. (1977), *Mechanics of the Mind* (BBC Reith
 Lectures, 1976), Cambridge University Press.
Blakney, R. B. (translator) (1955), *The Way of Life* (the *Tao Te
 Ching* by Lao Tzu), Mentor, New York.
Blofeld, J. (1970), *The Way of Power*, Allen & Unwin, London.
Blythe, R. H. (1942), *Zen in English Literature and the Oriental
 Classics*, Hokuseido Press, Tokyo.
Borges, J. L. (1964), *Labyrinths: Selected Stories and Other
 Writings*, Penguin Books, Harmondsworth, 1970.
Boston, R. (1974), *An Anatomy of Laughter*, Collins, London.
Braithwaite, R. B. (1953), *Scientific Explanation* (paperback ed.),
 Cambridge University Press, 1968.
Brown, G. Spencer (1969), *Laws of Form*, Allen & Unwin,
 London.
Bucke, R. M. Quoted in James (1902) and Happold (1963).
Bunyan, J. (1678), *Pilgrim's Progress*, Everyman's Library, Dent,
 London, 1966.

Cabell, J. B. (1919), *Jurgen*, Tandem, London, 1971.

Calvino, I. (1974), *Invisible Cities* (translation), Picador, Pan Books, London, 1979.

Campbell, J. (1949), *The Hero with a Thousand Faces*, Bollingen Series XVII, Pantheon Books, New York.

Campbell, K. (1970), *Body and Mind*, Macmillan, London.

Camus, A. (1942), *L'Étranger* (*The Outsider*, translation), Penguin Books, Harmondsworth, 1964.

Chandler, A. (1908), *Ara Coeli: An Essay in Mystical Theology*, 3rd ed., Methuen, London, 1909.

Chesterton, G. K. (1908), *The Man Who Was Thursday: A Nightmare*, Penguin Books, Harmondsworth, 1967.

Chesterton, G. K. (1929), 'The perishing of the Pendragons', in *The Wisdom of Father Brown*, Penguin Books, Harmondsworth, 1974.

Chuang Tzu. Quoted in Watts (1957).

Clark, J. H. (1970), 'A program for Patanjali', *New Society*, vol. 16, no. 408.

Clark, J. H. (1972), 'A map of inner space', in Ruddock, R. (ed.), *Six Approaches to the Person*, Routledge & Kegan Paul, London.

Clark, J. H. (1979), 'The varieties of ineffability', *Proceedings of a Colloquy of European Psychologists of Religion*, Catholic University, Nijmegen, The Netherlands.

Clark, J. M. and Skinner, J. V. (translators) (1963), *Meister Eckhart: Selected Treatises and Sermons*, Fontana, London.

Cohen, S. (1970), *Drugs of Hallucination*, Paladin, London.

Custance, J. (1951), *Wisdom, Madness and Folly*, Gollancz, London. Quoted by Happold (1963).

Dickens, C. (1864–5), *Our Mutual Friend*, Penguin, Harmondsworth, 1981.

Doel, D. (1973), 'A Psychological Study of the Concepts of Death, Despair and Rebirth', Ph.D. Thesis, University of Manchester. To be published as *The Perennial Psychology*, James Clarke, Cambridge, (in press).

Douglas, M. (1971), 'In the nature of things', in M. Douglas, *Implicit Meanings*, Routledge & Kegan Paul, London, 1975.

Eccles, Sir John C. (1977), *The Understanding of the Brain*, McGraw-Hill, New York.

Eckhart, Meister. *See* Clark, J. M. and Skinner, J. V. (1963).

Eliot, T. S. (1931), 'The Pensées of Pascal', in *Selected Prose*, Penguin Books, Harmondsworth, 1958.

Eliot, T. S. (1939), *The Family Reunion*, Faber & Faber, London, 1979.

Eliot, T. S. (1944), *The Confidential Clerk*, Faber & Faber, London, 1967.

Fischer, R. (1975), 'Cartography of Inner Space', in Siegel, R. K. and West, L. J., *Hallucinations: Behaviour, Experience, and Theory*, John Wiley, New York.

Fodor, J. A. (1981), 'The mind–body problem', *Scientific American*, vol. 244, no. 1.

Forsyth, R. (1978), *The BASIC Idea*, Chapman & Hall, London.

Fremantle, A. (ed.), (1964), *The Protestant Mystics*, Mentor, New York.

Freud, S. (1926), *The Question of Lay Analysis* (translation), in *Two Short Accounts of Psycho-Analysis*, Penguin Books, Harmondsworth, 1966.

George, F. (1979), *Man the Machine*, Paladin, London.

al-Ghazali. Quoted in Happold (1963).

Grahame, K. (1908), *The Wind in the Willows*, Methuen, London, 1959.

Graves, R. (1955), *The Greek Myths*, Penguin Books, Harmondsworth, 1980.

Green, C. (1968), *Lucid Dreams*, Institute of Psychophysical Research, Oxford.

Happold, F. C. (1963), *Mysticism: a Study and an Anthology*, Penguin Books, Harmondsworth, 1967.

Hartman, E. L. (1973), *The Functions of Sleep*, Yale University Press, New Haven.

Harvey, W. (1628), *Movement of the Heart and Blood in Animals, an Anatomical Essay*. Trans. by Franklin, K. J., Blackwell Scientific Publications, Oxford, 1957.

Herrigel, E. (1953), *Zen in the Art of Archery*, Routledge & Kegan Paul, London.

Hesse, H. (1927), *Steppenwolf*, Penguin Books, Harmondsworth, 1979.

Hesse, H. (1943), *The Glass Bead Game*, Penguin Books, Harmondsworth, 1980.

Hoffer, A. and Osmond, H. (1967), *The Hallucinogens*, Academic Press, New York.

Hofmann, A. (1955). Cited by Slater and Roth (1977).

Huxley, A. (1946), *The Perennial Philosophy*, Fontana, London, 1966.

Huxley, A. (1954 and 1956), *Doors of Perception* and *Heaven and Hell*, Penguin Books, Harmondsworth, 1971.

James, W. (1902), *The Varieties of Religious Experience*, Fontana, London, 1960.

Jaspers, K. (1913), *General Psychopathology* (translation), Manchester University Press, 1962.

John of the Cross, Saint. Quoted by Stace (1960).

Julien, R. M. (1978), *A Primer of Drug Action*, W. H. Freeman, San Francisco.

Jung, C. G. (c.1916), *Septem Sermones ad Mortuos* (translated by Baynes, H. G.), Stuart & Watkins, London, 1967.

Jung, C. G. (1921), *Psychological Types*, Routledge & Kegan Paul, London, 1971.

Jung, C. G. (1952), *Answer to Job*, Routledge & Kegan Paul, London, 1954.

Jung, C. G. (1961), *Memories, Dreams, Reflections* (translation), Fontana, London, 1972.

Kafka, F. (1930), *The Castle*, trans. Penguin Books, Harmondsworth, 1973.

Kaplan, B. (ed.), (1964), *The Inner World of Mental Illness*, Harper & Row, New York.

Koestler, A. (1954), *The Invisible Writing*, Macmillan, New York. Quoted in Stace (1960).

Krishnamurti. See Lutyens (1970).

Laing, R. D. (1960), *The Divided Self*, Penguin Books, Harmondsworth, 1970.

Lambert, G. (1975), *The Dangerous Edge*, Barrie & Jenkins, London.

Lao Tzu. See Blakney (1955).

Laski, M. (1961), *Ecstasy*, Cresset Press, London.

Lawrence, D. H. (1921), *Women in Love*, Ace Books, London, 1959.

Legge, J. (translator), (1963), *The I Ching, The Book of Changes*, Dover Publications, New York.

Lewin, K. (1936), *Principles of Topological Psychology*, McGraw-Hill, New York.

Lilly, J. C. (1973), *The Centre of the Cyclone*, Paladin, London.

Little, W., Fowler, H. W. and Coulson, J. (1962), *The Shorter Oxford English Dictionary*, 3rd ed. revised by Onions, C. T., Oxford University Press.

Lutyens, M. (ed.), (1970), *The Penguin Krishnamurti Reader*, Penguin Books, Harmondsworth.

Macquarrie, J. (1955), *An Existentialist Theology*, Penguin Books, Harmondsworth, 1980.

Mare, W. de la, (1979), *Collected Poems*, Faber & Faber, London.

Marshall, C. Quoted in Fremantle (1965).

Martin, B. (1981), *Abnormal Psychology,* 2nd ed., Holt, Rinehart & Winston, New York.

Maslow, A. (1968), *Toward a Psychology of Being,* Van Nostrand Reinhold, New York.

Miller, G. A., Galanter, E., and Pribram, K. H. (1960), *Plans and the Structure of Behaviour,* Holt, Rinehart & Winston, New York.

Mitchell, R. (1981), *Depression,* Penguin Books, Harmondsworth.

Monro, D. M. (1978), *Basic BASIC,* Edward Arnold, London.

Munro, H. H. See Saki (1911).

Nahal, C. (ed.), (1971), *Drugs and the Other Self,* Harper & Row, New York.

Nerval, G. de (1853), 'Sylvie', trans. in *Selected Writings,* Panther, St Albans, 1973.

Nicholas of Cusa. Quoted by Happold (1963).

Nicholson, D. H. S. and Lee, A. H. E. (1917), *The Oxford Book of English Mystical Verse,* Oxford University Press, 1969.

Nyanatiloka, (1950), *The Word of the Buddha,* 6th ed. revised, J. F. Rowny Press, Santa Barbara, California.

Oswald, I. (1970), *Sleep,* Penguin Books, Harmondsworth.

Otto, R. (1917), *The Idea of the Holy* (translation), Oxford University Press, 1946.

Patanjali. See Stephen (1957).

Poe, E. A. (1927), *The Works of Edgar Allan Poe,* Oxford University Press, London.

Postle, D. (1980), *Castrophe Theory,* Fontana, London.

Prabhavananda, S. and Isherwood, C. (translators), (1947), *Bhagavad-Gita,* Phoenix House, London, 1960.

Proust, M. (1913–27), *Remembrance of Things Past* (translation), Chatto & Windus, London, 1957.

Radin, P. (1956), *The Trickster: a Study in American Indian Mythology* (with commentaries by Kerényi, K. and Jung, C. G.), Routledge & Kegan Paul, London.

Reps, P. (1957), *Zen Flesh, Zen Bones,* Penguin Books, Harmondsworth, 1971.

Richard of Saint Victor. Quoted by Happold (1963).

Saint-Exupéry, A. de (1945), *The Little Prince* (translation), Penguin Books, Harmondsworth, 1971.

Saki (Munro, H. H.), (1911), 'The Music on the Hill', in *The Bodley Head Saki,* The Bodley Head, London, 1963.

Sartre, J.-P. (1938), *Nausea* (translation), Penguin Books, Harmondsworth, 1970.

Scientific American Book, (1979), *The Brain*, W. H. Freeman, San Francisco.

Scientific American Readings, (1980), *Mind and Behaviour*, W. H. Freeman, San Francisco.

Shakespeare, W. (1623), *Macbeth*, University Paperback, Methuen, London, 1972.

Shakespeare, W. (1623), *The Winter's Tale*, Signet Classic, New York, 1963.

Slater, E. and Roth, M. (1977), *Clinical Psychiatry*, 3rd ed. revised, Baillière, Tindall & Cassell, London.

Snow, C. P. (1934), *The Search*, Penguin Books, Harmondsworth, 1965.

Snow, C. P. (1964), *Corridors of Power*, Penguin Books, Harmondsworth, 1966.

Stace, W. T. (1960), *The Teaching of the Mystics*, Mentor, New York.

Stafford-Clark, D. and Smith, A. C. (1980), *Psychiatry for Students*, 5th ed., Allen & Unwin, London.

Stephen, D. R. (1957), *Patanjali for Western Readers*, 2nd ed., Theosophical Publishing House, London.

Stevenson, Y. (1976), *The Hot-House Plant: an Autobiography of a Young Girl*, Elek-Pemberton, London.

Sutherland, S. (1976), *Breakdown*, Paladin, London, 1977.

Teresa of Ávila, Saint, (1588), *The Life of Saint Teresa of Ávila by Herself* (translation), Penguin Books, Harmondsworth, 1957.

Traherne, T. Quoted in Happold (1963).

Underhill, E. (1911), *Mysticism*, Methuen, London.

Watts, A. W. (1957), *The Way of Zen*, Penguin Books, Harmondsworth, 1962.

Waugh, E. (1957), *The Ordeal of Gilbert Pinfold*, Penguin Books, Harmondsworth, 1980.

Wilson, C. (1956), *The Outsider*, Gollancz, London, 1970.

Wingfield, A. and Byrnes, D. L. (1981), *The Psychology of Human Memory*, Academic Press, New York.

Wood, E. (1959), *Yoga*, Penguin Books, Harmondsworth.

Yates, F. A. (1964), *Giordano Bruno and the Hermetic Tradition*, Routledge & Kegan Paul, London.

Yeats, W. B. (1937), *A Vision*, Macmillan, London.

Zeeman, E. C. (1976), 'Catastrophe theory', *Scientific American*, vol. 234, no. 4.

Index